WORLD LEADERS IN CONTEXT
CASTRO

John Griffiths
Senior Lecturer in History
at the Polytechnic of North London

Batsford Academic and
Educational Ltd   London

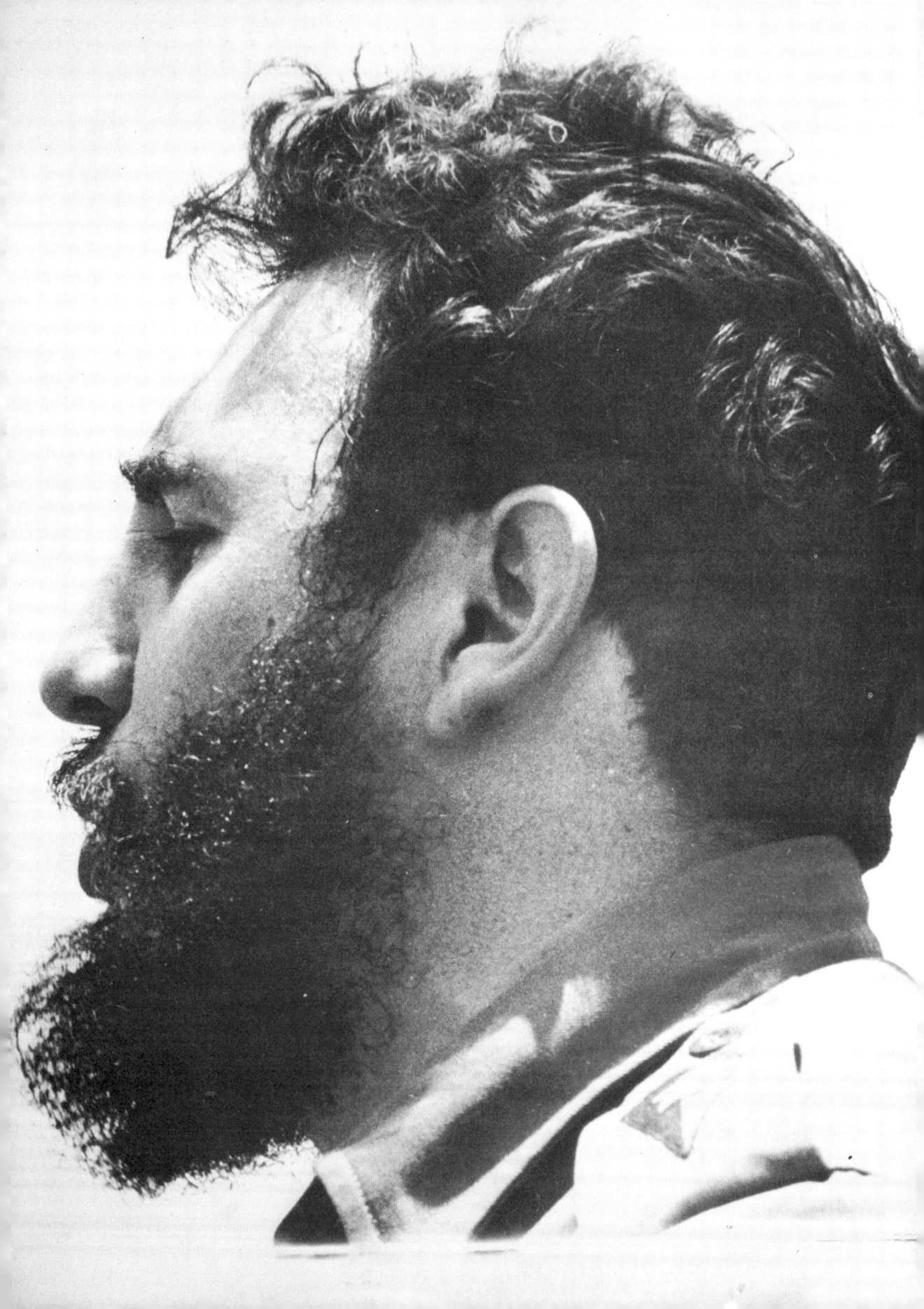

File Notes on Fidel Castro

1	**FAMILY NAME** Castro, Ruz		**GIVEN NAME** Fidel

2	**ALIASES & PSEUDONYMS**
	Alejandro (pseudonym in *El Acusador*, 1952) Alex (in letters from the Sierra Maestra)

3	**NATIONALITY**
	Cuban

4	**PLACE OF BIRTH** Biran, Oriente Province, Cuba	5	**DATE OF BIRTH** 13 August 1927
6	**FATHER** Angel Castro y Argis	7	**MOTHER** Lina Ruz Gonzalez

8	**BROTHERS & SISTERS**	
	Ramon (Mongo) Raul Teresa (Teresita) Angela and Juana	Half brother and sister, Lidia and Pedro-Emilio

9	**MARITAL DETAILS**
	Married Mirta Diaz Balart, 12 October 1948. Divorced 1955. (Reported married to Isabel Coto, in 1962.)

10	**CHILDREN**
	Fidel (Fidelito)

11	**DESCRIPTION**					
	HEIGHT	BUILD	HAIR	FACE	COMPLEXION	EYES
	6' plus	Broad		Bearded		

12	**MAJOR POLITICAL POSTS HELD**
	Commandante (Major) in Rebel Army/26th July Movement, Dec 1956–Jan 1959 Commander-in-Chief Armed Forces, Jan 1959– Prime Minister, Feb 1959–1976 Chairman of INRA (Agrarian Reform Institute), 1965– President of Council of State, 1976– Chairman of the Movement of Non-Aligned Countries, 1979–1984

© John Griffiths 1981
First published 1981

All rights reserved. No part of this publication may be reproduced, in any form or by any means, without permission from the Publisher

Typeset by Tek-Art Ltd, London SE20
and printed in Great Britain by
R.J. Acford Ltd
Chichester, Sussex
for the publishers
Batsford Academic and Educational Ltd,
an imprint of B.T. Batsford Ltd,
4 Fitzhardinge Street
London W1H 0AH

ISBN 0 7134 1924 5

For Linda, Nick and Emma who always stay behind.

Acknowledgment
I wish to thank the following for assistance given in the completion of this book; Cro. Jorge Bolaños, Cro. Cipriano Castro, Cro. Alcides Alberteris, and Cra. Sandra Castañer of the Cuban Embassy in London; Cro. Miguel Roa of Prensa Latina; Cro. Ricardo Rodriguez and the staff of ICAP, Havana.

All the illustrations in this book are from the Author's collection. The map on page 6 was drawn by Mr R. Britto.

Frontispiece: Fidel Castro, 1981.

Contents

Chapter One
Early Political Activities 7

Chapter Two
In the Sierra 15

Chapter Three
The Revolution in Power 25

Chapter Four
Building a New Society 39

Chapter Five
The Battle for the Ten Millions and
the Institutionalization of the Cuban
Revolution 49

Chapter Six
The Revolution Becomes Respectable? 57

Date List 71

Biographical Notes on
Fidel Castro's Contemporaries 77

Glossary 81

Some Suggestions for Further Reading 85

Visual Aids 87

Index 89

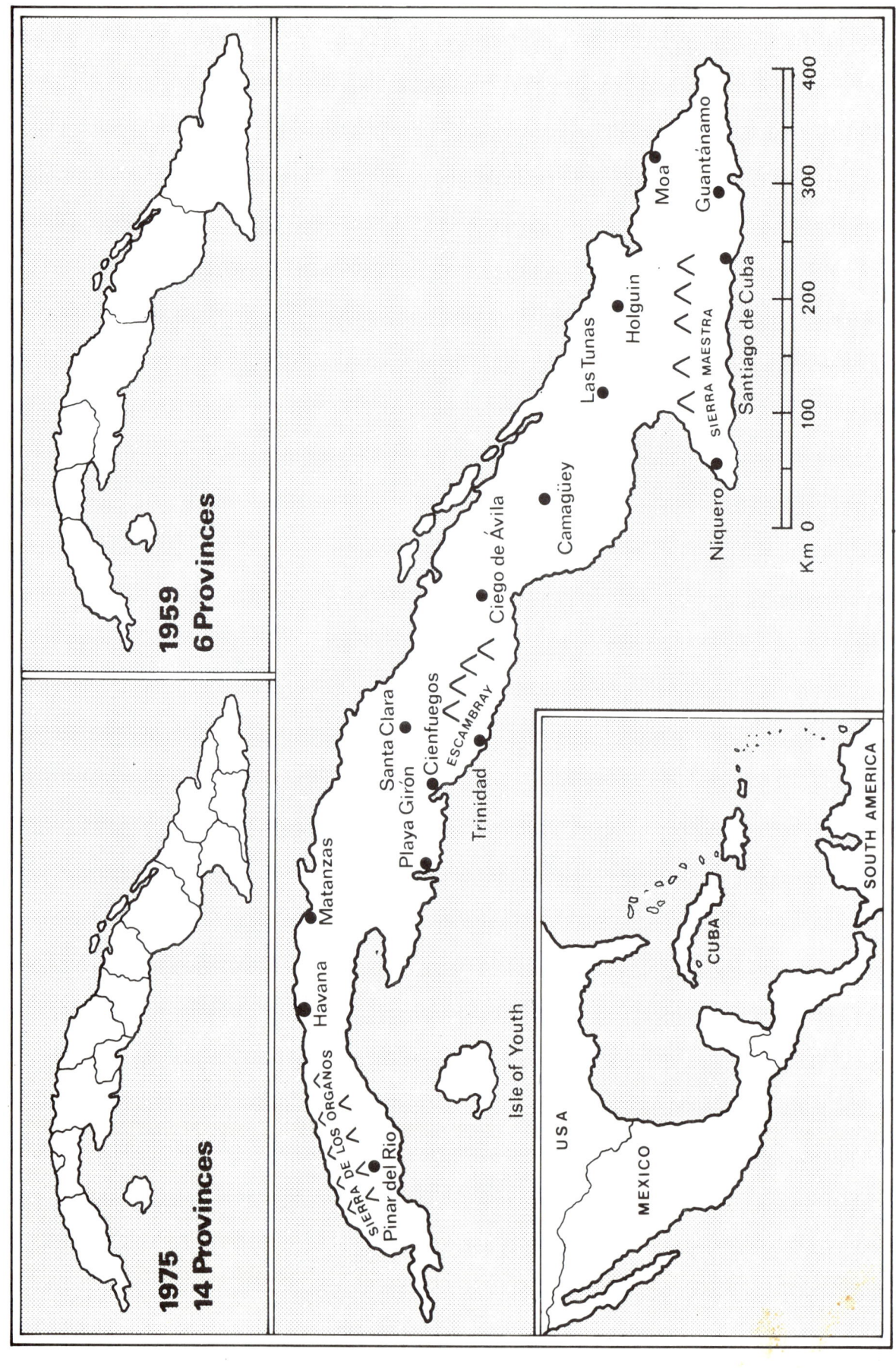

Chapter One

Early Political Activities

When I entered the University on finishing school, it was as the son of a landowner and, to make matters worse, as a political illiterate. And that landowner's son, who had been educated in bourgeois schools and had been subjected to U.S. propaganda, began to think there was something wrong with the system, that it didn't make sense.

Fidel Castro became involved in politics when he entered the University of Havana in 1945. During a visit to Chile in 1971 he spoke of the effect of his early life on his political thought:

Something must have had a bearing on my

1 Fidel Castro, sixth from the left, in the basketball team of the Jesuit Colegio de Belen, 1945.

developing the positive aspects we all have. That's why I consider myself lucky to have been the son of a landowner. As the son of a rising landowner, I at least had the advantage of living in the countryside and could mix with the peasants, with the humble people, who were all my friends. Some positive factors were developed at school; a concept of good and evil, just and unjust; and a certain spirit of rebelliousness against imposition and oppression led me to an analysis of society and turned me into what I later realised was a communist.

In the 1940s Cuba was going through one of its periodic bad times. The President, Grau San Martin, elected in 1944, had not delivered the hoped-for reforms. Rather, he had brought in one of the most corrupt regimes ever experienced in Cuba. Money for public works found its way into individuals' pockets, while money from gambling, prostitution and drugs was shared out among the police and government officials. Groups of gunmen — "pistoleros" — fought one another in the city's streets, even in the University.

Two years after joining University, Fidel Castro joined a new political party, the Orthodox Party, led by Eduardo Chibas, which was committed to "Nationalism, Anti-Imperialism, Socialism, Economic Independence, Political Liberty and Social Justice". But all these ends, it was hoped, would be achieved by legal, peaceful means.

During this time a rumour spread round the University that an invasion was about to be launched on the Dominican Republic to kick out the dictator, Trujillo. Although the plan was supposed to be secret, it was soon common knowledge throughout Havana. Fidel Castro was one of the first to come forward, and after a crash course in military training in Oriente Province, near his family home, he and over a thousand others went to a tiny island, Key Confite, one of the many hundreds that make up the Cuban archipelago, to await the order to attack.

It never came. The organizers of the attack, opportunists rather than revolutionaries, fell out among themselves and the Cuban Navy were ordered by the government to tidy up the affair by arresting all those waiting on Key Confite. Fidel Castro got away before the Navy arrived. The lesson of needing to be able to rely on others, learned in the Dominican Republic adventure, was not lost on him.

Back in Havana, he increased his political activities at the University to bring down the hated Grau government. He quickly came to the attention of the whole country through a somewhat bizarre plot. In early November 1947, with a fellow student, Lionel Soto, he went to Manzanillo, in Oriente, and after much persuasion, brought back to Havana the famous bell of Demajagua. This bell had tolled to signal the start of the hostilities against the Spanish, at the beginning of Cuba's War of Independence in 1868. The plan now was to ring the bell in Havana to let President Grau know that his time was up.

Unfortunately, when Castro and Soto got the bell back to Havana, it was stolen by supporters of the President. This only served to increase Castro's feelings against him and he expressed his anger forcefully at a rally at the University of Havana:

> Wasn't it Grau who spoke of national dignity, of the abandoned peasant and the hungry children? He promised land reform to the peasants, schools for the children and pay increases for teachers. None of these pledges have been fulfilled.

He was to make virtually identical charges against the next President, Batista, six years later.

Fidel Castro in Bogota — the "Bogotazo"

Fidel Castro's first experience of revolutionary upheaval came, not in Cuba, but by chance in Bogota, Colombia. He went there in 1948 as one of the Cuban representatives at the Latin American Student Congress. The Cuban delegation had barely unpacked when they were caught up in the pandemonium on the streets; an important Colombian political figure, Jorge Eliecer Gaitán, had been assassinated and the people had taken to the streets in a movement against the government.

Little for sure is known of Fidel Castro's activities during the "Bogotazo", though he is reckoned to have participated in an armed attack on the Presidential Palace. What we do know for sure is that he later had to seek asylum in the Cuban Embassy in Bogota and was subsequently taken out of the country in a plane-load of cattle going to Cuba. There is little doubt that his experience at the "Bogotazo" made a strong impression on him and, together with his University experience, guided his later action.

In 1949 he left the University — by now married, and with a son — to take up practice as a lawyer specializing in cases for workers and for the poor. He maintained contact with the University as well as continuing his work for the Orthodox Party, and he was constantly in conflict with the authorities. He was accused of being a trigger-happy gangster, an accusation often made against opponents of the government. But undeterred, he kept up his attacks on the government through whatever channels were open to him: in the press, at public meetings, and in the law courts.

The Orthodox Party suffered a major setback in 1951, when its leader Eduardo Chibas, committed suicide. Fidel Castro kept up his links with the Party and in 1952 appeared to stand a good chance of gaining a seat in the Congress, Cuba's parliament. He was a popular public figure because of his support for the poor and unjustly treated in his legal work and because he had exposed numerous examples of graft and corruption by the government.

But his hopes, along with everyone else's, were dashed when, on 10 March 1952, Fulgencia Batista took power in a military coup. Fidel Castro was quick to denounce him, writing in *El Acusador* ("The Accuser"), a simple duplicated newspaper, three days later:

2 Fulgencia Batista who took power in a coup on 10 March 1952, so depriving Fidel Castro of the opportunity to be elected in the Cuban Congress.

> We have suffered misrule for many years awaiting the constitutional opportunity to exorcise the evil. And now you, Batista . . . appear with your poisonous remedy, tearing the Constitution into pieces when there are only two months to go before arriving at our goal by adequate means.
>
> It would be good to overturn a government of embezzlers and murderers. That is what we were attempting to do by following the civic road, and with the backing of public opinion and the aid of the masses. What right do you have to substitute with bayonets those who yesterday robbed and killed people?

With legal opportunities to make changes now closed off to him, Fidel Castro began to examine other ways of bringing them about.

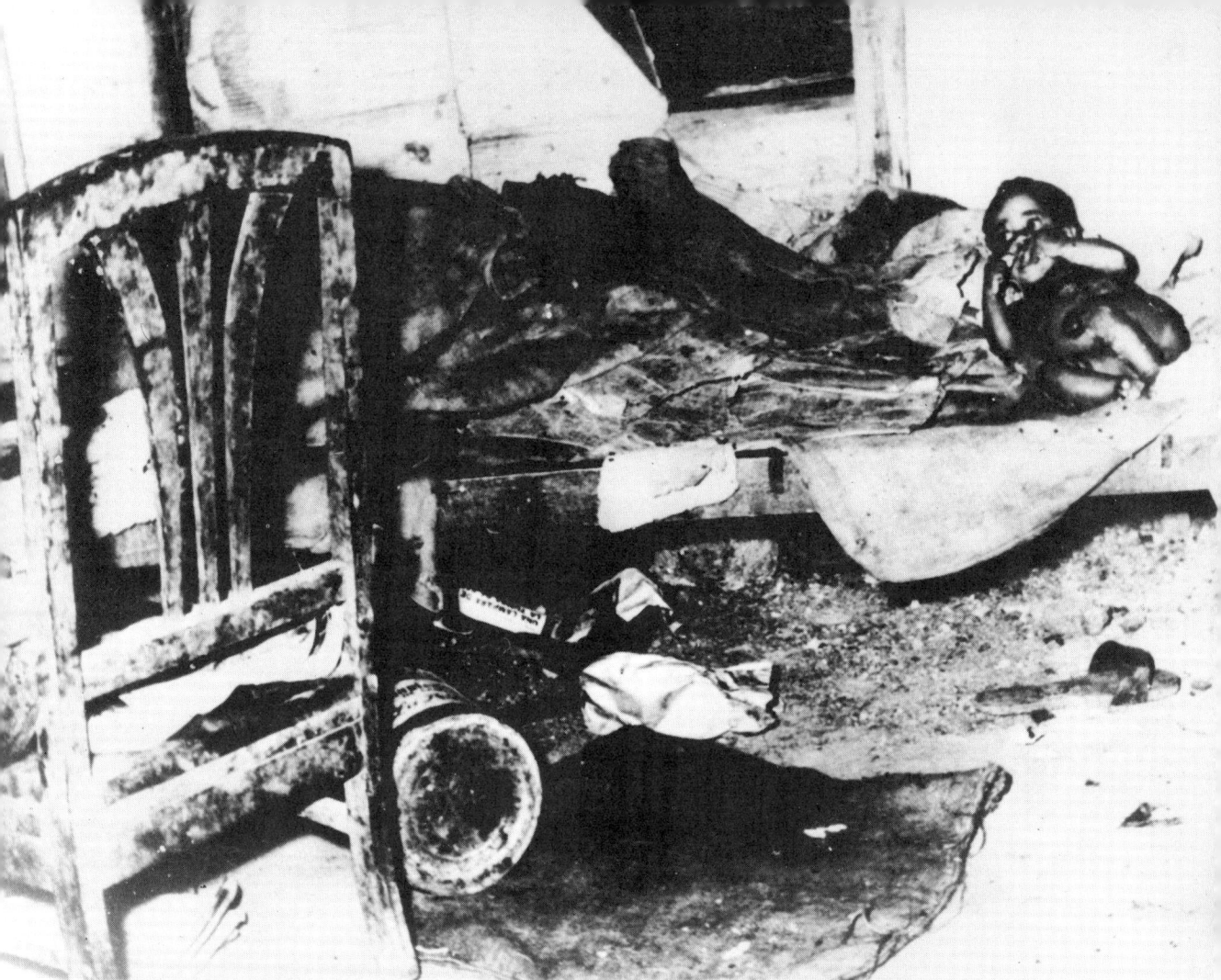

3 Poor insanitary housing was just one of the problems plaguing Cuba in the 1950s, which Fidel Castro was determined to remedy.

In fact, he admitted in a speech in July 1976 that

> Some of us, even before 10 March 1952, had come to the conclusion that Cuba's problems had to be solved in a revolutionary manner and that power had to be seized at a given moment with the masses and with arms and that socialism was the objective.

The Attack on the Moncada

26 July 1953 is now an important anniversary in Cuban history. It is seen as the date on which the armed phase of the revolutionary struggle against Batista began, ending in victory on 1 January 1959.

On 26 July a group of men, led by Fidel Castro, attacked the Moncada Barracks in Santiago de Cuba. Moncada was chosen for the attack because it was the second most important military base in Cuba, after Havana, and far enough away from the capital for it to be difficult for reinforcements to arrive quickly. It had other advantages: it was in the south of Oriente Province, close to the Caribbean Sea, surrounded by mountains with few access points, making its defence ideal once the city had been captured. The nearby mountains, the Sierra Maestra, from where Fidel Castro was later to lead the Revolution, would provide a base and haven for the Revolutionaries if the fighting dragged on. Perhaps more important, Oriente had been in the forefront of opposition to the Spanish in the nineteenth century; its people had a history of rebellion and could be counted upon to support the fight against Batista.

The plan was to take two military targets by surprise, the Moncada, with 134 men, and the nearby garrison at Bayamo, with 28 men; and then to take the Headquarters of the National Police and the Cuban Navy Headquarters in Santiago. While all this was going on, the "Moncada Manifesto" would be broadcast — the final step in setting up a liberated area in Santiago, from where a "revolutionary storm" would be unleashed throughout the whole island.

Sunday was the day chosen for the attack. It was the day of celebration of Santa Maria during the annual Carnival, still held in Santiago, which would be at its peak. Only a handful of rebels knew the details of the plan. They spent their time organizing their "troops", hiding them away in safe houses in the city, their movements disguised by the hundreds of other strangers in Santiago for the Carnival. "Some of my friends are coming from Havana for the Carnival," was how the arrival of Fidel Castro's group was disguised.

A small house was rented — ostensibly as a chicken farm — at Siboney, a short distance outside Santiago. Here, in the early hours of 26 July some 130 men and 2 women gathered to learn the details of the planned attack. Fidel Castro addressed them:

> Within a few hours you may be either the victors or the vanquished, but no matter what — listen well, comrades — this movement will be victorious. If you win tomorrow, what Marti aspired to will be done sooner. If the opposite happens, this action will serve as an example to the people of Cuba, and from this people will come, others ready to die for their country.
>
> You know the plan's objectives. It is, without doubt, a dangerous plan and anyone who leaves this house with me tonight must do so of his own free will. There is still time for you to reconsider.
>
> Anyway, some of you will have to remain, since we are short of weapons. All those ready to go step forward. The order of the day is not to kill except in case of extreme necessity.

(from *Granma*, Cuba's national newspaper, 9 July 1967)

Ten decided not to proceed. This depletion of their ranks did not pose problems, but there were difficulties, as one of the group told *Granma* later:

> When Fidel tried on the largest uniform it still wouldn't fit him. Looking at himself in the mirror, he worried that he wouldn't look like a soldier of the regime, which role we were playing in attacking the garrison.

(Pedro Trigo, *Granma*, 18 June 1967)

The rebels divided their forces into three. Fidel Castro was to personally direct the attack, at the head of the largest force, whose task was to take the Barracks. The second group, led by Raul Castro, was to occupy the Palace of Justice; and the third group, of 21 men and 2 women, led by Abel Santamaria, would take the city hospital. The two women, Haydée Santamaria and Melba Hernandez, were to remain at the hospital to care for the wounded. It was crucial that the attacks should take their targets by surprise.

An account of what happened was given by one of the attackers:

> During the trip from Siboney to Santiago little was said. The first three cars headed up the street leading to Gate 3 just before dawn. We immediately spotted the two soldiers in a garrison patrol car . . . parked in front of the gate. Our first car passed it; our men greeted the patrol who responded but kept an eye on them.
>
> At that moment, a soldier who appeared to be straggling in from the carnival came alongside the patrol car, just a few metres from us, which had just arrived.
>
> On orders from Fidel, Arcos leapt from the car to grab the soldier but slipped and

4 The Moncada Barracks showing signs of the armed attack made on it by Fidel Castro and his group on 26 July 1953.

fell. The soldier went for his gun but was shot by one of the men in the car behind ours.

The men in the first car had already disarmed the two guards at the gate, which was in our hands, and the chain had been dropped. Some of the rebels had already entered the garrison. The patrol, which saw the taking of the gate in astonishment, turned on us when the shot rang out. Seeing the soldier fall, they opened up on our car, point blank, then drove swiftly off. These were the shots that gave the alarm and destroyed the element of surprise. Already we were the target of enemy fire.

Fidel, standing in the street despite the firing, ordered us to advance on the garrison, but the barrage of fire prevented us. We were forced to take shelter wherever we could find it: behind the cars, between the near-by houses, behind the walls of the garrison itself.
(Reinaldo Benitez Napoles, 1967)

Some of Castro's troops were already inside the garrison holding troops prisoner; those outside quickly took up defensive positions. Fidel Castro tried unsuccessfully to reorganize his group, but with the element of surprise lost and — more bad luck — a considerable number of his group lost in the unfamiliar streets of Santiago, he ordered the withdrawal. The attack on Bayamo had been equally dogged by bad luck, equally unsuccessful, and its attackers were similarly in retreat.

Fidel's plan was to retreat quickly to the small town of El Caney, near Santiago, capture the Rural Guard Garrison there, and, with stolen weapons, take to the mountains. But their driver took the wrong road and they

5 Fidel Castro, on the right, after his capture and arrest following the unsuccessful attack on the Moncada Barracks.

returned to the farm at Siboney where they divided into three groups to take to the mountains and to continue the fight from there.

On 1 August Fidel Castro and his companions were captured as they slept in a country farmhouse. They were taken to the main prison in Santiago, where Fidel's brother Raul and other rebels who had been captured immediately after the Moncada attack were being held prisoner. They were lucky not to have been killed on sight as other members of their group had been.

Two months later the "Moncadistas" were brought to trial. Fidel Castro, however, was kept separate from the rest, and news was brought to the court that he was very ill and in hospital. It was only when a nurse from the hospital smuggled out a letter from Fidel Castro, explaining a plan to have him killed, that he was finally put on trial, though still not publicly.

"History Will Absolve Me"

His trial was a great opportunity for Fidel Castro to turn the tables on Batista, and he rapidly became not the accused but the accuser. He condemned the authorities for the barbarity of their reprisals against the "Moncadistas", many of whom had been cruelly tortured before being killed. He linked the action of the rebels he had led with the struggle of the nineteenth-century Revolutionaries for Cuban independence from Spain. And he spoke of José Martí as "the intellectual author of the 26 July".

Wearing a borrowed gown that was too small for him, Fidel Castro conducted his own defence, in which he listed the groups of people for whom he was struggling against Batista's unjust and corrupt regime:

> Seven hundred thousand Cubans without work who want to earn their daily bread honestly without having to emigrate in search of a livelihood.
>
> Five hundred thousand farm labourers inhabiting miserable shacks, who work four months a year and starve for the rest of the year, sharing their misery with their children who have not an inch of land to cultivate, and whose existence should inspire compassion, were not so many hearts made of stone.
>
> Four hundred thousand industrial workers whose retirement funds have been embezzled, whose benefits are being taken away, whose homes are wretched quarters, whose salaries pass from the hands of the boss to those of the usurer, whose future is pay-reduction and dismissal, whose life is eternal work and whose only rest is the grave.
>
> One hundred thousand small farmers who live and die working on the land that is not theirs looking at it with sadness as Moses did the Promised Land, to die without possessing it, who like feudal serfs have to pay for the use of their parcel of land by giving up a portion of their product; who cannot love it, beautify it, improve it or plant a tree on it because they never know when a constable will come with the Rural Guard to evict them from it.
>
> Thirty thousand teachers and instructors who are so dedicated, so selfless and necessary to the better destiny of future generations and who are so badly paid and treated.
>
> Five thousand young professionals: doctors, engineers, lawyers, vets, teachers, dentists, chemists, journalists, painters, sculptors, etc. who come from school with their diplomas, anxious to work and full of hope, only to find themselves at a dead end and with all doors closed.
>
> These are the people, the ones who know misfortune, and therefore are capable of fighting with endless courage.

He went on to detail what changes would have been made had their plan for Revolution been successful:

> The problem concerning land; the problem of industrialisation; the problem of housing; the problem of unemployment; the problem of education; and the problem of the health of the people; these are the six problems we would have taken immediate steps to solve, along with the restoration of public freedoms and political democracy.
>
> I warn you, I have just begun! If there is in your heart a vestige of love for justice, listen to me closely. I know that I will be silenced for many years. I know that the regime will try to suppress the truth by all possible means. I know that there will be a conspiracy to sink me into oblivion. But my voice will not be stilled; it gathers strength in my breast even when I feel most alone and I want to give it, deep in my heart, all the warmth that callous cowards deny it.

It was a passionate defence lasting over two hours, and ending defiantly with the words:

> Condemn me, it doesn't matter. History will absolve me.

Fidel Castro subsequently pieced the speech together from memory while he was in prison — he was sentenced to 15 years — and it was smuggled out and published clandestinely as a book entitled *History Will Absolve Me*.

The attack on Moncada was more than a failure, but one undoubted result was to draw the attention of the whole nation to a new, young, revolutionary movement and, once again, to Fidel Castro, who was to emerge as the undeniable political and military leader of the Revolution. Three years after Moncada, many of the participants were again involved in revolutionary activity, this time as members of the Rebel Army, led by Fidel Castro and named appropriately the 26th July Movement — M26J.

Chapter Two

In the Sierra

Prison

The survivors of Moncada were sent to El Presidio, the model prison on the Isle of Pines (the next largest island after the mainland) on 13 October 1953. Fidel Castro arrived three days later. Even in prison he was determined to carry on the fight against Batista. His brother Raul said later:

> From the beginning Fidel told us that our imprisonment should be combative and we would acquire a rich experience from it, experience that would help in the continuation of the struggle once we were freed.

One of the first things the "Moncadistas" did was to set up their own school where they could learn basic subjects, as well as politics, to prepare for their eventual release. However, Fidel Castro was singled out for special treatment and put into solitary. He described the experience to Barbara Walters, an American journalist, in a long interview for television in 1977:

> I spent many months in solitary. I had the company of the mosquitoes and my cell was in front of the place where the bodies of those who died in prison were kept before they were buried. Every so often I had the company of a corpse, and, every day, that of millions of mosquitoes. But I always had some book or other; I studied and I adapted. The fact that I detest solitude doesn't mean I'm not able to stand it.

He "stood it" by making himself an oil-lamp by which to read. He kept up contact with his friends and sympathizers outside, whom he constantly encouraged to keep up the struggle

6 Fidel Castro's official prison photograph and number.

which he had begun. To one friend he wrote:

> What should be considered before starting a battle for freedom is not how many weapons the enemy has, but the virtue to be found in the people. If in Santiago one hundred courageous youths fell it means only that in the whole of Cuba there are 100 thousand ready to die. Look for them and you will find them. The masses are ready, they only need to be shown the right road.

Despite his imprisonment, Fidel Castro did not at first lose his optimism and enthusiasm, issuing campaign orders from his cell. To Melba Hernandez, one of the two women involved in the Moncada attack, he wrote:

> Propaganda cannot be abandoned for a single minute, as it is the soul of every struggle.
>
> The work of our people here and abroad must be co-ordinated.
>
> To know how to wait, said Marti, is the great secret of success.
>
> Deal with the people carefully and with a smile. Defend our point of view without making unnecessary enemies. There will be enough time later to crush all the cockroaches together. Do not be discouraged because of anything or anyone.

But it was not long before the strain of imprisonment began to have its effect on him; he became angry and disillusioned:

> Any situation cannot be harder. I do not know if it is the mental torture of being alone, or seeing the incredible things that are happening. How can it happen in Cuba that [I be put into solitary confinement] with absolute impunity, and amidst the great indifference of almost everyone.

His state of mind was not helped by the news that his wife, Mirta Diaz Balart, had been receiving money from Batista through her brother, a government minister. Shortly afterwards he learnt that she was divorcing him. At the same time, his revolutionary ideas were not receiving much attention, as the Cuban people's hopes for change were directed towards the ballot box.

Batista felt secure enough in May 1954 to repeal his own martial law regulations and free a few political prisoners, though not the "Moncadistas", and then he went ahead with "free and honest" elections. His opponents were weak and divided and he was able to get elected by default: nobody else bothered to run against him. Throughout the election Fidel Castro insisted that his followers carried on with their propaganda for armed struggle, and their views met with some response. The election revealed the weakness of Batista's position, which was based solely on remaining in power for as long as possible by whatever means.

Taking advantage of Batista's "liberal" phase, the supporters of the "Moncadistas" mounted an appeal for their release, backed by many of Cuba's most prominent individuals. After a year of campaigning they managed to get Fidel Castro and the twenty-nine men of his group freed. But, even in 1977, in his American TV interview, Fidel Castro was at pains to point out who was really responsible for their freedom:

> It wasn't Batista who set us free. It was the people with their movement; it was the masses with their demands that coincided with Batista's interest in holding a mock election. He couldn't hold it while we were in jail so to further his plans and his interests, he released the few survivors of the attack on the Moncada after murdering more than 70 of our comrades.

Fidel Castro was once again in the public arena after twenty-two months of imprisonment in Santiago and the Isle of Pines, and again he could use the press for propaganda purposes for his political campaign. *Bohemia*, Cuba's most well-read weekly magazine, was quick to interview him, and on 22 May 1955 reported his words:

Now we are free we assert without any reservation that since we are not professional agitators, if the present circumstances were to change and if the regime were to respect the rights of all, we would change the tactics of our struggle.

Yet Castro knew well enough that only violence would bring down Batista, so he planned accordingly. He made his position clear in the pages of *Bohemia* once again:

> Six weeks after our release, after seeing the intentions of the governing clique — ready to remain in power for twenty years, at the instance of flatterers and opportunists without conscience — I no longer believe in the effectiveness of general elections. All doors to civilian struggle are closed, the only solution left is to follow the example given in 1868 and 1895 [for armed revolution].

Too effective in his political campaign against Batista, Fidel Castro was banned from making public speeches and was followed wherever he went. He soon found such constraints impossible to bear, and on 7 July 1955 he went into exile in Mexico. He openly sent a letter to leading political figures in Cuba explaining:

> I am leaving Cuba because all doors of peaceful struggle have been closed to me. As a follower of Marti, I believe the hour has come to take rights and not to beg for them. I will reside somewhere in the Caribbean. From journeys such as these one does not return, or else returns with the tyranny beheaded at one's feet.

In Mexico

The sole purpose of leaving Cuba was to organize a return, to set the country on the road to revolution. This would be brought about by the 26th July Movement, M26J, which had been formed after Fidel Castro's release from prison. He explained the nature of the movement in the 1st Manifesto to the

7 José Martí looks down from the wall as Fidel Castro speaks to a group of Cuban exiles in New York in 1955 during a fund-raising tour of the USA.

people of Cuba, from Mexico in August 1955:

> The 26th July Movement is formed without hatred for anyone. It is not a political party but a revolutionary movement. Its ranks are open to all Cubans who sincerely desire to see political democracy re-established and social justice introduced in Cuba. Its leadership is collective and secret, formed by men of strong will who are not accomplices of the past.

The effect of this statement was immediate. Throughout Cuba "26" was seen everywhere, painted on walls, on cars, on buses; young people especially responded to the revolutionary call. Outside Cuba, Fidel Castro whipped up support and very necessary funds.

"Patriotic Clubs of the 26th July" were set up throughout the USA to raise money for the movement, which was used to organize and train men who were to invade Cuba to begin the revolution.

Colonel Alberto Bayo, a Cuban living in Mexico, who had previously fought in the Spanish Civil War, was given the job of military instructor. In a farm outside Mexico City, he disciplined his "troops", taught them guerilla techniques, sabotage and marksmanship — everything necessary for their survival during the armed struggle against Batista.

It was in Mexico that Fidel Castro met Ernesto Che Guevara, a young Argentinian doctor, who was to play an important role in the Revolution. Che remembered that first meeting in his book *Reminiscences of the Cuban Revolutionary War*:

> I met him on one of those cold Mexican nights and I remember that our first conversation dealt with the subject of international policy. Within a few hours of our meeting — in the early morning hours — I had already become one of his future revolutionaries.

While in Mexico Che wrote a poem about Fidel:

> Let us be off
> ardent prophet of the dawn,
> Along, hidden unbarbed paths
> to liberate the green crocodile you love so well.
>
> Let us be off
> to defeat outrage with the insurgent stars of Marti
> stamped on our foreheads.
> Let us swear to secure victory
> or meet death.

The "green crocodile" was, of course, Cuba.

For Batista, Fidel Castro and M26J represented a very real threat. Cuban agents of the President encouraged the Mexican authorities to harass the group and even to assassinate Fidel Castro. In June 1956 Fidel Castro and Ramiro Valdes were arrested:

> On that occasion I could easily have died accidentally. I remember that Ramiro and I walked through this street when we became aware that a number of cars were following us, inside of which were several suspicious individuals. We thought they were Batista's assassins. I told Ramiro to follow me and did not realise when I reached the corner where there was a building under construction, that he had been arrested. I thought my back was safe and saw a group of armed men get rapidly out of a car to try to intercept me. I hid behind a column and when I tried to take out my automatic pistol, a policeman who had taken Ramiro's place put his 45 pistol in the back of my head.

All the Cubans were arrested for the possession of illegal firearms and breaking Mexican immigration laws. Although most were released after about a month, the Mexican authorities kept up a continuous harassment. This was a desperate time for the Revolutionaries; their arms had been confiscated, their money was used up. Against his better judgement, because it could have put him under a political obligation, Fidel Castro accepted funds from Prio Soccaras, a former President of Cuba, which enabled their preparation to continue.

With the money Fidel bought an old yacht called *Granma* from an American family living in Mexico. It was in bad condition and, at 23 metres long, designed to carry only ten passengers. Yet this craft was to take all the Revolutionaries to Cuba. Speed was important with the Mexican authorities at their heels.

Before leaving Mexico, Fidel Castro met with all the underground leaders of M26J in Cuba and agreed a national uprising and general strike, to coincide with their landing in the country. Then, on 25 November, in a storm so fierce that all sailing had been banned, the

Granma left Mexico, with eighty-two men aboard.

Che Guevara described their journey:

> The course we'd chosen took us in a big curve around the South of Cuba, skirting Jamaica, and the Cayman Islands, to bring us to the disembarkation point somewhere near the town of Niquero in the [former] province of Oriente. Our plans were quite slow to materialize. On the 30th [November 1956] we heard on the radio the news of the uprisings in Santiago de Cuba which had been organised by our great Frank Pais, who reckoned that they'd coincide with the arrival of the expedition. The following day, December, 1st, during the night, we set our course direct for Cuba, desperately searching for the Cabo Cruz Lighthouse, without water, food or fuel. At two in the morning, the night black and stormy, the situation was alarming. The lookout were coming and going, scanning the horizon in vain for a glimmer of light. Roque, a former naval lieutenant, went up to the small upper bridge again to search for the Cabo light, lost his footing and fell into the water. Shortly after starting off again we saw the light, but the wheezy running of the boat made the last hours of the journey seem endless. It was daytime when we reached Cuba at a place called Belic on Las Coloradas beach. A coastal sailing boat spotted us and telegraphed the news to Batista's army. We'd scarcely disembarked, in a great hurry, and taking with us only what was absolutely necessary, and were setting off into the swamp when we were attacked by enemy planes. Of course, once in the mangrove swamp we couldn't be seen by the planes but the army of the dictatorship was already on our heels.
> (from *Reminiscences of the Cuban Revolutionary War*)

Marching by day and night to avoid capture, the rebels set up camp on 5 December, near a sugar cane field. Exhausted and with no sentries, they were surprised by Batista's troops. Many were shot and others killed when the troops set fire to the cane. The rebels took off in several groups towards the mountains. Fidel Castro tried to make his way to the house of a friend:

> By day we hid under the fallen sugar cane leaves because planes flew over us incessantly. We ate sugar cane and used the dew on the leaves to quench our thirst. Then we decided to get out of there. At night we cautiously moved out using the stars to guide us.

Thinking that he had successfully dealt with the threat posed by the rebels, Batista called in his troops.

In the Sierra

During the next few days the survivors from the *Granma* straggled in to a jubilant welcome. Raul Castro described his arrival:

> ... not knowing what had happened to the rest of the comrades — I led what was left of my platoon to the Sierra Maestra.
> After 15 or 20 days I found Fidel with two other comrades. Only two comrades! Three men armed with two rifles. The first thing he said to me was: "How many rifles do you have?" and I answered: "Five". Then he said "With these seven rifles we will win the war." It was difficult for us to have as much faith as he had, although we did learn through his faith.

Of the original group only thirty armed men remained — hardly cause for Fidel Castro's apparent optimism. A few days later they marched to Turquino Peak, Cuba's highest point, where Fidel Castro shouted to the winds: "We have won the war." It was to be two more hard years before that was to be a reality.

Despite Batista's claim that the Revolutionaries were dead, they were, in fact, preparing for war against him. They had set up a

8 In the Sierra Maestra after his return to Cuba in December 1956 in *Granma*, Fidel Castro draws a plan of campaign in the dust. Che Guevara is on the left of the picture.

headquarters; were soon in contact with underground groups throughout Cuba; and, wisely, kept their presence secret from Batista's troops. The peasant peoples of the Sierra Maestra, historically a rebellious group, supported Fidel Castro, supplying his men with food and supplies, for which they were paid and given protection. Schools and clinics were set up for the benefit of the peasants as much as for M26J's troops.

Life in the Sierra Maestra was hard, but it had its positive side, as Fidel Castro was to point out later:

9 On Turquino Peak, the highest point in Cuba in the Sierra Maestra, from which Fidel Castro shouted "We have won the war".

The struggle in the Sierra Maestra taught us a great deal about every aspect of life. It taught us how to fight, how to solve difficult problems and developed the best virtues among our men during those 2 years of struggle.

I wonder what would have happened if we had scored a victory in 1953, with much less experience to our credit and also with much greater odds against us.

Fidel Castro has even described this as one of the "happiest" times of his life; especially when compared with the responsibilities of government. In his TV interview with Barbara Walters in 1977 he said:

I think that, in a way, it was one of the happiest times. Mainly because the struggle was a very hard one; living conditions were very difficult. It was an all-out struggle for survival. I believe that in those circumstances man gives the best that's in him. The risks that were faced in war, the effort that had to be made ... and, of course, everything was simpler then. Also I feel at home when I'm in action — maybe because I'm mainly a man of action. That stage included a number of political and organisational aspects but there was also plenty of action. That's why I think it was one of the best periods that any of us had.

Early in 1957 Batista again suspended all civil rights in Cuba. The rebels responded by attacking one of his army outposts, the La Plata Barracks, in Oriente Province. Che Guevara described the battle:

We prepared to attack with the 22 available weapons. It was an important moment, for we had few bullets; we had to take the barracks no matter what, for otherwise we would spend all our ammunition and remain practically defenseless.

This was the Rebel Army's first victorious battle. This and the following battle were the only occasions in the life of our troop when we had more weapons than men.
(from *Reminiscences of the Cuban Revolutionary War*)

Apart from the military success of the attack, the propaganda value was enormous. Fidel Castro and the revolutionary cause were once again in the news despite Batista's attempts to deny his existence. This was made more difficult, anyway, by the interview of Fidel

21

Castro in the Sierra Maestra by the journalist Herbert Mathews, that was subsequently published in the *New York Times*:

> Fidel Castro, the rebel leader of Cuba's youth, is alive and fighting hard and successfully in the rugged, almost impenetrable fortress of the Sierra Maestra, at the southern tip of the island. President Fulgencia Batista has the cream of his army around the area, but the army men are fighting a thus-far losing battle to destroy the most dangerous enemy General Batista has yet

10 Fidel Castro explains the working of a rifle to Haydee Santamaria, on the left, who participated in the attack on the Moncada, and Celia Sanchez who became Fidel Castro's trusted secretary and companion.

> faced in a long and adventurous career as a Cuban leader and dictator.
> (*New York Times*, 28 February 1957)

Batista at first denied the interview had ever taken place, but was forced to eat humble pie when photographs showing the journalist and the rebels' leader were published. To give Mathews an inflated image of their numbers, Fidel Castro ordered his men to create a lot of activity in the camp, marching in and out. At the time, he had only eighteen men with him. Mathews went away with the idea that there were nearly ninety. He also went away with a high impression of Fidel Castro:

> The personality of this man is overwhelming. It was easy to see that his men adored him and also to see why he has caught the imagination of the youth of Cuba. Here was an educated, dedicated fanatic, a man of ideals, of courage and remarkable qualities of leadership.

But, whatever Fidel's claim of high morale among his men, in reality the situation was bleak: hard physical and mental conditions made it difficult to attract and keep new members. And Batista, forced to acknowledge the presence of the rebels, stepped up his attacks on them, from the ground and the air. Their ranks were successfully infiltrated; on one occasion Fidel Castro shared his blanket with a traitor armed with grenades and other weapons he had brought into the camp to use against Castro. In the towns, too, morale was low and in desperation a plot was hatched to get rid of Batista in one go.

The Attack on the Presidential Palace

In March 1957 a group of fifty men from different political organizations, mainly from the Revolutionary Directorate (DR), launched

11 "El Loquito", The Nut, was designed by the cartoonist Nuez in 1958 to break Batista's strict censorship. All mention of what was happening in the Sierra Maestra was banned, so here Nuez has Fidel Castro driving the No. 30 bus that runs to the Havana suburb of "la Sierra". "El Loquito" 's hat is made of censored newsprint.

a surprise attack on the Presidential Palace in Havana. The guards were rapidly overcome and the attackers reached the first floor and the office of Batista, who, hearing the commotion, escaped by a secret exit. In this retreat the attackers were mown down by Batista's army. Few survived.

To coincide with the attack, another group took over Radio Reloj, Cuba's main radio station, to announce Batista's death. On their way out of the building, this group was unlucky in meeting a police patrol; a fight ensued and their leader, José Antonio Echeverria was killed.

From the mountains, Fidel Castro denounced this action as counterproductive:

> . . . a useless spilling of blood. The life of the dictator does not matter. I condemn these procedures. Nothing is solved by them. Here in the Sierra Maestra is where they should come to fight.

Batista's reaction was to unleash a harsh retribution upon the resistance to the regime, which resulted eventually in the virtual annihilation of many town-based groups. And so the way was left clear for the leadership of M26J in the Sierra. Fidel Castro became indisputably the leader of the armed struggle against Batista.

The Scent of Victory

After March 1957 the position improved for the rebels. New members flocked to join them and they could count on political support from all political groups and individuals opposed to Batista.

In May another successful military attack was launched against the garrison of El Uvero. After this Batista closed down all the small barracks in Oriente, concentrating his troops in the towns. He was clearly on the run. Over the next year the Revolutionaries caused much disruption and there were several strikes, until on 24 May 1958 Batista launched a massive army attack on the rebels. Battle began, and the rebels made rapid progress. Fidel Castro gave a "Report on the Offensive" over Radio Rebelde, their own radio station, on 18 August 1958:

> After 76 days of fighting at the No. 1 Front in the Sierra Maestra, the Rebel Army stopped and virtually wiped out the best forces of the tyranny, inflicting one of the biggest defeats ever suffered by a modern army, trained and supplied with all kinds of military material, at the hands of non-professional military forces who were limited to an area surrounded by hostile forces and lacking planes, artillery and regular means of communication and food.
>
> If the war lasts six more months, the

army will fall apart completely. It can only face up to the situation ahead with the support of all the population. And the opposite is the case: all the population supports and backs the rebellion . . .

The Rebel Columns will advance on all fronts and nothing and nobody can stop them. If one commander falls he will be replaced by another; if a man is killed his spot will be filled by someone else.

The people of Cuba must prepare to aid our fighters. Any City or part of Cuba can become a battlefield in the coming months. The civilian population must be ready to face the privations of war with resolution. The courage shown by the people of the Sierra Maestra — where even the children help our men — who have gone through 20 months of war with incomparable heroism, must be emulated everywhere, by all Cubans, so we may be truly free, cost what it may. In this way, we will be true to the promise of Antonio Maceo when he said, "The Revolution will continue as long as there is a wrong to right."

In the early hours of 1 January 1959, giving those close to him little warning, Batista left Cuba. He had been militarily and politically defeated by the rebel army led by Fidel Castro. Why had it been successful? Speaking in 1971 to a huge crowd in Revolution Square, Havana, on the eighteenth Anniversary of the Attack on Moncada, Fidel Castro explained:

> Theoretically speaking, victory was impossible. And yet, in the prisons, in the most remote places, faith in victory was never lost. Neither on July 26th, after the attack on the Moncada; nor on December 5th, after the Granma expedition was scattered; nor when there were only two, ten, twelve of us left. Never did we lose our conviction and confidence in victory. The theoreticians would have said, "Such a revolution is impossible". The theoreticians would have said, "Such a war is impossible".
>
> But life teaches us that an impossible thing — or a thing that seems impossible — is often possible in the realities of life. It is possible especially when the people are armed with ideas, when revolutionary ideas are taken up by the masses. Then all those things that seemed impossible become possible.

But, as Fidel Castro said many times during the course of the Revolution, it was easier to win the war against Batista than to win the war against underdevelopment and backwardness. That was to be his next task.

Chapter Three

The Revolution in Power

Setting up a New Regime

As Batista flew out of Cuba to a comfortable exile and Fidel Castro approached Santiago de Cuba, politicians in Havana plotted to ensure that a revolution did not occur. Fidel Castro moved immediately:

> This is Radio Rebelde at the door of Santiago de Cuba. Dr. Fidel Castro is now coming to the microphones to make an important announcement.
> F.C.: "Regardless of the news coming from the Capital, our troops are not to cease fire, no matter what. Our forces are to continue their operations against the enemy on every front. A truce will be accepted only in the case of those garrisons that want to surrender.
> It appears as if a coup d'état has taken place in the Capital. The people are to remain on the alert and obey only the instructions issued by the General Command.
> The Dictatorship has crumbled as a result of the crushing defeats dealt in the past few weeks but this does not mean that the Revolution has already triumphed."

Looking back, in a speech in March 1973, Fidel Castro explained why it was necessary to continue to fight:

> This military pseudo-coup to which Batista had agreed, was staged on the night of December 31st, or rather in the early morning hours of January 1st [1959] and it was necessary to react quickly in the face of events. We had to destroy all illusions that a coup d'état could mean the triumph of the revolution. We had to put the people on the alert.

However, on taking Santiago a few hours later, Castro had no doubts as to the final outcome. In a speech to the people of Santiago who had gathered to welcome the Rebel Army from the Sierra Maestra, he made clear his objectives:

> This time the Revolution will not be frustrated: it will not be as it was in 1895 when the Americans came and became the masters of the country when they intervened at the last moment and even Calixto Garcia, who had fought for 30 years, was prevented from entering Santiago de Cuba; it will not be as it was in 1933, when the people began to believe that the Revolution was being made when Mr. Batista came, betrayed the Revolution, installed himself in power and established a ferocious dictatorship; it will not be as it was in 1944, the year in which multitudes were incited into believing that at last the people had come to power and actually those who had come to power were thieves. Neither thieves nor traitors, nor interventionists: this time it *is* Revolution.

12 Fidel Castro and Camilo Cienfuegos, on the left, on their triumphant entry into Havana, 8 January 1959.

The revolutionary history of the nineteenth century is continuously stressed like this in the speeches of Fidel Castro, who sees the success of the Cuban Revolution as being the culmination of "100 years of struggle".

Once Santiago had been taken, and also Havana, by Che Guevara and Camilo Cienfuegos, and it was clear that the people would have nothing to do with another coup d'état, Fidel Castro set out to drive in triumph from Santiago through the country to Havana in the east. He received a hero's welcome in every village and town he passed through. On 8 January 1959 he arrived in Havana and that evening made his first speech to the people of the town. He chose Camp Columbia, Batista's main army barracks, as venue:

> I think that this is a decisive moment in our history. The tyranny has been overthrown. Our joy is overwhelming, but there is much to do. Let's not fool ourselves into thinking that from now on everything is going to be easy. Maybe from now on everything will be even more difficult.
>
> I was asked what kind of troops I'd prefer to lead, and I said, I'd prefer to lead the people, because the people are invincible and it was the people who won the war. We had no Army, no Navy, no tanks, no planes, no guns, no military academies or recruiting or training units, no divisions, no companies or platoons — but we had the people's trust and, with that alone, we were able to win the battle for freedom.

From then on Fidel Castro regularly made speeches, sometimes lasting for hours at a

13 Flanked by Camilo Cienfuegos and surrounded by "doves of peace", Fidel Castro makes his first public speech in Havana at Camp Columbia, the former military barracks of Batista's troops, 8 January 1959.

time, listened to by thousands of Cubans, whatever the weather. These speeches were crucial in the 1960s, for they were the main channel of information from the government to the people, and a way for the government to gauge the mood of the people. Che Guevara described the effect of Fidel Castro's speeches on the crowds:

> Fidel is a past master at this; his particular mode of integration with the people can only be appreciated by seeing him in action. In the big public meetings, one can observe something like the dialogue of two tuning forks whose vibrations summon forth new vibrations each in the other. Fidel and the mass begin to vibrate in a dialogue of growing intensity which reaches its culminating point in an abrupt ending crowned by our victorious battle cry.
> (from *Man and Socialism in Cuba*)

Some form of government needed to be set up, as Fidel Castro explained to a group of University students in Chile in 1971:

> A de facto revolutionary government was set up and the laws were enacted by decree. The Constitution was put into effect, a series of modifications of it were introduced and the Council of Ministers was invested with the power to make laws. This made things easier for our country. These were very special circumstances.
>
> Once the Revolutionary Government was established, the laws were enacted by decree. And, in this situation, some vestiges of the bourgeois state — such as the administration apparatus — remained. Remained? Some vestiges of the bourgeois state remain even now in Cuba. I only wish we could say there weren't any.
>
> But Revolution made greater progress in the political field and in the field of mass organisations than in that of creating an apparatus to replace the old bourgeois state with all its ministries and so forth.

Then the new leaders of Cuba looked to solve the country's major problems: unemployment; the poor living conditions in country and town of almost half the 5 million population because of high rents and electricity costs; illiteracy and lack of schools; ill health and shortage of hospital beds; the unfair system of land ownership.

Relating Cuba's problems in 1959 to the United Nations General Assembly the following year, Fidel Castro made it clear that he blamed the United States government:

> Public utilities, electricity and telephone services all belonged to the United States of America's monopolies. A major portion of the banking business, of the importing business, all the oil refineries, the greater part of the sugar production, the best land in Cuba, and the most important industries in all fields belonged to American companies. The balance of payments, from 1950 to 1960, had been favourable to the United States of America, with regard to Cuba, to the extent of one billion dollars.
>
> One billion dollars in ten years! This poor and underdeveloped Caribbean country, with 600,000 unemployed, was contributing greatly to the economic development of the most highly industrialised country in the world.
>
> We surely cannot be blamed [for the unemployment and illiteracy]. Until that moment, none of us had anything to do with the destiny of our country; until that moment, those who had something to do with the destiny of our country, were the rulers, who served the interests of the monopolies. Did anyone hinder them? No one. Did anyone trouble them? No one. They were able to do their work, and there we found the result of their work.

This was bound to put Cuba and the USA on a collision course.

US/Cuban Relations

Did problems with the United States of

America's government arise from the very first moments? No. Is it perhaps that when we reached power we had the intention of getting into international trouble? No. No revolutionary government wants international trouble when it comes to power. What a revolutionary government wants to do is concentrate its efforts on solving its own problems.

In his speech to the UN in 1960, Fidel Castro complained first that the USA had immediately welcomed the "murderers" who fled from Cuba after the victory of the Revolution. But it was when the Cuban revolutionary government had begun to take its first steps to deal with some of its own problems that relations with the USA had worsened:

The first thing [the Revolution] did was to lower the rents paid by families by fifty per cent.

Then another law was passed cancelling the concessions which had been granted by the tyranny of Batista to the telephone company, an American monopoly. Thus began the first conflict with the American monopolies.

The third measure was the reduction of electricity rates, which were the highest in the world. Then followed the second conflict with the American monopolies. We were beginning to appear communist; they were beginning to daub us red because we had clashed head on with the interests of the United States of America's monopolies.

Then followed the next law, an essential and inevitable law for our country: the Agrarian Reform Law. Was it a radical Agrarian Reform? We think not. It was a reform adjusted to the needs of our development, and in keeping with our own possibilities of agricultural development. In other words, it was an agrarian reform which was to solve the problem of landless peasants, the problem of supplying basic foodstuffs, the problem of rural unemployment, and which was to end, once and for all, the ghastly poverty which existed in the countryside.

And that is where the first major difficulty arose.

Then the problem of payment arose. Notes [from the United States of America] rained on our government. They never asked us about our problems, not even out of sheer pity, or because of the great responsibilities they had in creating these problems. A sympathetic attitude towards our needs? Certainly not. All the talks by the representatives of the government of the United States of America centred upon the telephone company, the electric company, and the land owned by the American companies.

How could we solve the problem of payment? Of course, the first question that should have been asked was what we were going to pay with, rather than how.

We were not one hundred per cent communist yet. We were just becoming slightly pink. We did not confiscate land; we simply proposed to pay for it in twenty years; in bonds, which would mature in twenty years at four and a half per cent.

But in Cuba it was not only the land that was the property of the agrarian monopolies, but the largest and most important mines were also owned by those monopolies. Cuba produces, for example, a great deal of nickel. All of the nickel was exploited by American interests. Exempt from all taxes what were those companies going to leave Cuba? The empty, worked-out mines, the impoverished land, and not the slightest contribution to the economic development of our country. And so the revolutionary government passed a mining law which forced those monopolies to pay a twenty-five per cent tax on the exportation of minerals.

Then began a new period of harassment of the Revolution. The attitudes of the Revolution had to be finished. Punitive actions of all sorts — even the destruction of those insolent people — had to follow the audacity of the revolutionary government.

Economic reprisals by the USA began, as well as more aggressive tactics:

> One afternoon an aeroplane coming from the north flew over one of our sugar refineries and dropped a bomb. This was a strange and unheard-of event but we knew full well where the plane had come from. On another occasion, another plane flew over our sugar-cane fields and dropped a few incendiary bombs. These events which began sporadically continued systematically.

American concern with the Cuban Revolution was that it was becoming taken over by Communism, as the *New York Times* of 24 June 1959, reported:

> The Revolution may be like a watermelon. The more they slice the redder it gets. So says one American businessman here [in Cuba], one of a growing number of residents who are becoming increasingly disenchanted with the policies of Fidel Castro's revolutionary government. Cuba's controversial new agrarian reform law, which will expropriate large landholdings and divide them up among landless Cuban country people, has crystallised American opposition [in Cuba] to Prime Minister Castro.

This was even though, only a month before, on 21 May, Fidel Castro had been quite specific about his political position, in a televised speech:

> Our revolution is neither capitalist nor Communist. We want to liberate man from dogmas, and free his economy and society, without terrorising or binding anyone. We have been placed in a position where we must choose between capitalism that starves people, and Communism that resolves the economic problem but suppresses the liberties so greatly cherished by man.
>
> Our revolution is not red, but olive green, the colour of the rebel army that emerged from the heart of the Sierra Maestra.

But America's preoccupation with the threat of Communism in Cuba continued, and was shown by the then President of the United States, Dwight D. Eisenhower, and by his Vice-President (later to be President himself), Richard M. Nixon, who was under no doubt that Fidel Castro "was a Communist or under Communist domination".

But was he? In his speech to the UN General Assembly in September 1960 Fidel Castro again stressed the opposite, pointing out that while the US press were painting Cuba "a red peril", the Cuban government had not yet been able to establish diplomatic or commercial relations with the USSR. And Nikita Kruschev, then Chairman of the USSR, reinforced this point in his memoirs:

> There is a story that characterises the situation in Cuba and Fidel Castro's role at that time. The leaders of the Cuban Revolution go up to heaven; St. Peter comes to meet them as God's official representative and orders them all to line up. Then he says, "All Communists three steps forward!" [Che] Guevara steps forward. Raul [Castro] steps forward; so does someone else. But all the rest, including Fidel, stay in line. Peter glares at Fidel and shouts, "Hey, you, the tall one with the beard! What's wrong, didn't you hear what I said? All Communists three steps forward!"

(from *Kruschev Remembers*, 1971)

The point of this story is that St Peter and everyone else considered Fidel Castro a Communist; Fidel himself did not.

Faced with an unsympathetic USA, Fidel Castro had to turn to the only other large market and source of credit: that was the USSR. In February 1960 Anastas Mikoyan, the first Deputy Minister of the USSR, visited Cuba with a Soviet Trade Fair. Cuba was already selling sugar to the USSR, from an agreement signed the previous autumn. As a result of Mikoyan's visit, Cuba and the Soviet Union signed an agreement whereby Cuba would sell 5 million tons of sugar over a five-year period, for which the USSR would pay 80 per cent in goods and 20 per cent in hard currency. A US economics journal pointed out:

> The agreement says specifically that Russia will trade heavy machinery to the Cubans. The island needs tractors, farm equipment and industrial machinery, which it has been unable to purchase on credit terms from American companies.

In spite of these contracts with the Soviet Union, Fidel Castro still sought friendly, mutually respectful relations with the USA. It was not to be. President Eisenhower, encouraged by Vice-President Nixon, had asked the Central Intelligence Agency (CIA) to draw up a plan of invasion of Cuba, using disaffected Cubans living in the USA.

The Bay of Pigs Invasion

On 4 March 1960 a French ship, the *La Coubre* which was carrying Belgian armaments to Cuba, exploded in Havana Harbour, killing seventy-five persons and injuring more than thirty more. Fidel Castro was suspicious that the US government was responsible, as it had tried, by diplomatic methods, to prevent Cuba from getting the arms. At a mass rally in honour of those who had died, he voiced his suspicions, although he did not explicitly accuse the US government:

> In order to make that statement, we would need material evidence, which we do not have.
>
> But I do say that we have a right to think that those who have so far failed to achieve their purpose might well have tried to achieve their purpose by other means. So it is among those with motives that we must look for those who brought about the toll of Cuban lives yesterday afternoon.

On subsequent occasions Fidel Castro has been more specific in his accusations against the USA for its involvement in the disaster.

Fidel Castro and the other Cuban leaders were justifiably concerned that the US government might try to topple their government as they had done in Guatemala in 1954. These fears were increased when the US government cut its quota of sugar from Cuba in June 1960.

In the summer of 1960, the CIA began training Cuban counter-revolutionaries and mercenaries for their invasion plans. Economic and diplomatic pressure against Cuba increased. There was no doubt of Fidel Castro's prestige inside Cuba, as the American *Wall Street Journal* of 27 September 1960 indicated:

> Few reasonable neutral observers [in Cuba] doubt that Castro could win an honest election if it were held tomorrow. . . . Today, most workers and peasants who are the majority of Cuba's people, must be counted Castro's supporters.

During the election campaign in the USA in 1960, both Senators John F. Kennedy and Richard Nixon vied with each other to produce the most aggressive statement on Cuba. Senator Kennedy called Cuba a "Communist state", in "the grip of a Communist dictatorship", which had been "permitted to arise only 90 miles" from US shores. It comes as no surprise, therefore, that on his election, Kennedy persisted with the previous administration's plans to invade Cuba and get rid of Fidel Castro. The plans were an open secret in Cuba as well as in the USA.

On 27 February 1961 the *Wall Street Journal* reported:

> It is no secret that this country [United States of America] is already furnishing

14 A show of determination on 16 April 1961 at the funeral of those killed in the air attack near Havana that preceded the invasion of Cuba at the Bay of Pigs.

weapons and supplies to anti-Castro forces in Central Cuba's Escambray mountains and training counter-revolutionaries in Florida and Guatemala.

On 19 March 1960 Cuba demanded, for the fourth time in the past year, a United Nations hearing to discuss the threat of invasion. But

> One quiet, clear dawn, on April 15, 1961, Yankee bombers bearing Cuban insignia attacked our air bases where a few rickety old planes with barely a half-dozen pilots, constituted our Air Force. With unparalleled cynicism, the United States representatives declared in the United Nations that those planes were part of our own Air Force that had rebelled.

This was how Fidel Castro described the beginning of the attack, on its fifteenth anniversary in 1976.

On the day of the attack, in 1961, faced with immediate protests from the Cuban government, Adlai Stevenson, the US representative at the UN, put his country's case forcefully:

> No United States of America personnel participated in the incident. The attack was carried out by Castro's planes which took off from their own airfields.
>
> I reiterate President Kennedy's statement to the effect that under no circumstances will there be United States intervention in an aggression on Cuba.

He was to find later that he had been misled.

The next day, 16 April, at the funeral of those killed in the attack, Fidel Castro spoke to a crowd of ten thousand people:

> This is why they cannot forgive us; that we are here, right under their noses, and that we have made a socialist revolution right under the very nose of the United States.

This was the first time that the Cuban Revolution had been characterized by Fidel Castro as "socialist". He went on:

15 Fidel Castro, who took personal command of Cuban forces during the Bay of Pigs invasion, leaps from a tank at the height of the fighting.

The United States delivered the bombs, the planes, and trained the mercenaries. The yankees are trying to deceive the world, but the whole world knows that attack was made with yankee planes, piloted by mercenaries paid by the US Central Intelligence Agency.

As he finished his speech, Fidel Castro was handed a note reporting that a US warship was moving towards Cuba.

The invasion proper started on 17 April. Fidel Castro's account continues:

16 Some of the 1,189 prisoners captured at the Bay of Pigs. They were later exchanged for medicines and baby foods. President John F. Kennedy of the USA refused to exchange tractors.

We only had eight old planes and six pilots. We didn't even have spare parts for those planes. In their raid, the United States of America had destroyed some of our planes, even though we had some anti-aircraft defences. However, our few remaining pilots and planes were in the air when dawn came on the 17th [April, 1961]. They were headed for Playa Giron [Bay of Pigs] — the objective was the invasion ships. Our planes lost no time in sinking practically all of the invasion fleet. After their ships had been sunk we still had to contend with the invaders.

Seventy-two hours after it had begun, the invasion at the Bay of Pigs, or Playa Giron, as it is known to the Cubans, was over. In the United States, President John Kennedy, in the White House, felt personally responsible for the counter-revolutionaries who had been killed and the 1,189 taken prisoner in the affair. A few days after the defeat at the Bay of Pigs, the first defeat in his career, he asked one of his aides: "How could I have been so stupid as to let them go ahead?

The Literacy Campaign

1961 was also the time of another different kind of battle in Cuba. While the fight was raging on the beaches at Playa Giron, young literacy workers — "Brigadistas" — were living and working in the remote areas of Cuba, struggling to teach illiterate people how to read and write. In the First Manifesto issued from the Sierra Maestra, Fidel Castro had announced the intention of the revolutionary government to deal definitely with the problem of illiteracy:

> The provisional government must adjust its mission to the following programme: immediate initiation of an intensive campaign against illiteracy, and civic education emphasising the duties and rights of each citizen to his society and country.

The schools set up in the mountains were the first steps taken in this direction.

17 A Cuban cartoon at the time of Giron, the Bay of Pigs, showing each royal palm tree, the symbol of Cuba, representing a gun to the invaders.

In 1960 at the United Nations headquarters in New York, Fidel Castro made public Cuba's plans.

> Next year our people propose an all-out offensive against illiteracy, with the ambitious goal of teaching every illiterate person to read and write. Organisations of teachers, students and workers — the entire population — are preparing themselves for an intensive campaign and within a few months Cuba will be one of the first countries in the Americas to be able to claim that it has not a single illiterate inhabitant.

Half-way through the campaign, after Playa

Giron, Fidel Castro himself took over the running of it, appearing nightly on television to give a progress report. With maps and diagrams he appeared like a general reporting on a war. And war was being waged against one of Cuba's most pressing problems.

But the literacy campaign was not just about teaching people to read and write; it had a politicizing function as well. Young people from the towns were coming face to face with backwardness and underdevelopment for the first time in their lives. And if the peasant people of Cuba were to contribute to the country's political, economic and social development, they must first of all be literate. Fidel Castro made the connection between politics and education in a speech to voluntary Literacy Teachers in September 1961:

> The countries that are the most exploited economically and the most oppressed politically are the countries that have the most illiterates. Only a revolution is totally capable of changing the education scene in a country because it also totally changes the political scene, the economic scene, and the social scene. The levels of ignorance and illiteracy, the numbers of children not attending school, are really frightful in the economically exploited nations. Why? Because in reality there is not the least interest in remedying these conditions.

18 A "Brigadista" looks on as the peasant family with whom he lived complete their writing exercise during the 1961 Literacy Campaign. Not possessing a desk, they use an upturned box instead.

Working from the premise: "If you know, teach; if you don't know, learn", the whole of Cuba was caught up in the literacy campaign, so that at the end of 1961, it could be claimed that Cuba had indeed got rid of illiteracy. The final test of all those who had studied throughout the year was to write a letter to Fidel Castro. This is one of them:

> Dr. Fidel Castro,
> Comrade,

This letter is to express to you my deepest thanks, so deep that I have no words to explain to you my great joy at having carried out and been successful in the literacy campaign and fulfilled the promise you made before the whole world. Also, I feel very happy because now I have my opportunity to carry out my desire which is to study.
Yours sincerely,
Amada Nieve.

Everything for our Socialist Revolution.

Fatherland or Death.

The October Missile Crisis

On Tuesday morning, October 16th, 1962, shortly after nine o' clock, President Kennedy called and asked me to come to the White House. He said only that we were facing great trouble. Shortly afterwards in his office, he told me that a U2 [reconnaissance plane] had just finished a photographic mission and that the intelligence

19 At the end of the Literacy Campaign, December 1961, students march in triumph through the streets of Havana to be addressed by Fidel Castro.

community had become convinced that Russia was placing missiles and atomic weapons in Cuba.

This was the beginning of the Cuban Missile Crisis — a confrontation between the two great atomic nations, the United States of America and the U.S.S.R., which brought the world to the abyss of nuclear destruction and the end of mankind.

This was how President Kennedy's brother Robert began the story of the Cuban Missile Crisis of 1962, in his book *13 Days, the Cuban Missile Crisis*.

After the Bay of Pigs invasion of 1961 President Kennedy had kept up contact with Cuban exile groups committed to the elimination of Fidel Castro and the Cuban Revolution. The US government was concerned at the establishment of a Marxist regime so close to its shores, for Fidel Castro had announced

INTERMEDIATE RANGE BALLISTIC MISSILE BASE IN CUBA

(Labels on photograph: PROB NUCLEAR STORAGE BUNKER; BATCH PLANTS; PRE-FAB CONSTRUCTION MATERIALS; LAUNCH PAD; CONTROL BUILDING; PROTECTED VEHICLE POSITION; LAUNCH PAD)

20 U2 photograph showing missile sites in Cuba September 1962.

on the eve of the Bay of Pigs attack that the Cuban Revolution was going to follow a "socialist" path to development, a point he had repeated the following May Day.

In December 1961 he made his famous statement that: "I am a Marxist and shall remain one until the end of my life." This put the Cuban Revolution firmly in the socialist camp, alongside the Soviet Union.

In the autumn of 1962 a much-publicized exercise by the United States of America, involving 7,500 marines, 4 aircraft carriers, 20 destroyers and 15 landing ships was planned for the Caribbean. The aim was to liberate a mythical country, "the republic of Vieques", ruled by a dictator Ortsac (to be read backwards!). To Fidel Castro, after the attack on the Bay of Pigs, it was further evidence of US aggression against Cuba.

By October 1962, when the United States

21 Fidel Castro at the height of the 1962 October Missile Crisis.

received the photographic evidence of nuclear missile sites on Cuba, and the "Missile Crisis" began, President Kennedy was under severe pressure to "do something" about Cuba, and so events moved rapidly. After intense and secret activity, Kennedy spoke to the American people on television on 22 October 1962:

> This government has maintained the closest surveillance of the Soviet military build-up on the island of Cuba. Within the past weeks, unmistakeable evidence has established the fact that a series of offensive missile sites is now in preparation on that imprisoned isle. The purpose of these bases can be none other than to provide a nuclear strike capability against the Western Hemisphere.

He went on to say that this constituted a change in the status quo between the USA and the Soviet Union and was quite unacceptable. A blockade was to be introduced around Cuba to prevent the introduction of any further missiles and bombers. He finished his address with an appeal to the Cuban people:

> Finally I want to say a few words to the captive people of Cuba, to whom this speech is being directly carried by special radio facilities. I speak to you as a friend, as one who knows of your deep attachment to your fatherland, as one who shares your aspirations for liberty and justice for all. And I have watched and the American people have watched with deep sorrow how your nationalist revolution was betrayed and how your fatherland fell under foreign domination. Now your leaders are no longer Cuban leaders inspired by Cuban ideals. They are puppets and agents of an international conspiracy which has turned Cuba against your friends and neighbours in the Americas — and turned it into the first Latin American country to become a target for nuclear war — the first Latin American country to have these weapons on its soil.
>
> Many times in the past the Cuban people have risen to throw out tyrants who destroyed their liberty. And I have no doubt that most Cubans today look forward to the time when they will be truly free — free from foreign domination, free to

22 Anastas Mikoyan, Deputy Prime Minister of the Soviet Union, in a tense meeting with Fidel Castro following the October Missile Crisis, 1962.

choose their own leaders, free to select their own system, free to own their own land, free to speak and write and worship without fear of degradation.

The diplomatic exchanges that then followed were directly between President Kennedy in the United States and Chairman Kruschev in the USSR, much to the annoyance of Fidel Castro. The Soviet Union was not prepared to go to war over its missiles in Cuba, although it disagreed with the USA over the nature of its assistance to Cuba. On 28 October 1962 Nikita Kruschev wrote to President Kennedy:

> The Cuban people want to build their life in their own interests without external interference. This is their right, and they cannot be blamed for wanting to be masters of their own country and disposing of the fruits of their own labour. The threat of invasion of Cuba and all other schemes for creating tension are designed to strike the Cuban people with a sense of insecurity, intimidate them, and prevent them from peacefully building their new life.
>
> The Soviet Government decided to render assistance to Cuba with means of defence against aggression — only with means for defence purposes.

In an earlier letter Kruschev had indicated to President Kennedy that:

> If assurances were given that the President of the United States would not participate in an attack on Cuba and the blockade lifted, then the question of the removal or the destruction of the missile sites in Cuba would then be an entirely different question. Armaments bring only disasters.

This became the basis of an unpublished agreement between the USA and the USSR, which Fidel Castro described to US journalists in 1979, during another "Caribbean Crisis" caused by the presence of Soviet troops in Cuba:

> When a settlement of the October Crisis was reached, an agreement between the USSR and the United States was reached by virtue of which the Soviet Union decided to withdraw all those weapons in exchange for a guarantee that Cuba would not be invaded.

While the USA was pledged not to carry out a direct attack on Cuba, however, Fidel Castro pointed out that "the imperialists"

> reserved the use of other forms of aggression: during those years they especially stepped up their economic blockade against our country and all their political and diplomatic manoeuvres against Cuba — which still continue.

At the time of the October Crisis in 1962 Fidel Castro would not allow observers to inspect the missile sites in Cuba unless the US government agreed to five points, including the evacuation of the Guantánamo marine base in Cuba, the end of economic aggression against Cuba, and the cessation of all aid to counter-revolutionary groups. The US government was not prepared to do so.

Chapter Four

Building a New Society

Breaking out of Underdevelopment

Fidel Castro was only thirty-two years old when he swept into Havana in 1959. Most of the Revolutionaries with him, who were to exert such an influence on the future course of Cuba's history, were also young. Few, if any, had any training in economics. But they all shared the same commitment: to get rid of the inequalities between town and country, get away from Cuba's reliance on one product, sugar, and set the wheels of development moving.

The first years of Revolution were ambitious times, and the young Revolutionaries were optimistic about solving Cuba's economic problems in a short period of time. Fidel Castro sounded optimistic when he spoke to the United Nations in 1960:

> The Cuban Revolution is changing what was yesterday a land without hope, a land of poverty and illiteracy, into one of the most advanced and developed in this continent.
>
> The revolutionary government, in just twenty months, has created 10,000 new schools. In this brief period it has doubled the number of rural schools that had been created in fifty years. In this brief period of time [we] have built 5,000 homes in the rural and urban areas. Fifty new towns are being built at this moment.
>
> Today our people are receiving the assistance of hundreds of doctors.
>
> Agricultural production in our country has been able to perform an almost unique feat, an increase in production from the very beginning. . . . Production was maintained through co-operatives, thanks to which we have been able to apply the most modern technical methods to our agricultural production.
>
> And all this social welfare work — teachers, housing, and hospitals — has all been carried out without sacrificing the resources that have been earmarked for development. At this moment the revolutionary government is carrying out a programme of industrialisation of the country, and the first plants are already being built.

But the ambitious industrialization plans were a failure. Expensive new factories rotted in the countryside, for Cuba was without the raw materials and the technological know-how to make them a success.

Che Guevara, in an article in *International Affairs* published in London in 1964, wrote of the Revolutionaries' mistakes in trying to achieve development:

> Our first error was the way we carried out diversification. Instead of embarking upon diversification by degrees we attempted too much at once. The sugar cane areas

were reduced and the land thus made available was used for cultivation of new crops. But this meant a general decline in agricultural production. The entire economic history of Cuba had shown that no other agricultural activity would give such returns as those yielded by the cultivation of sugar cane. At the onset of the revolution many of us were not aware of this basic economic fact, because of the idea connecting sugar with our dependence on imperialism and with the misery in the rural areas, without analysing the real causes. Unfortunately, whatever measures are taken in agriculture, the results do not become apparent until months, sometimes years, afterwards. That is why the reduction of the sugar cane areas made between the middle of 1960 and the end of 1961 has resulted in the lower sugar cane harvests of 1962 and 1963.

The second mistake made was that of dispersing our resources over a great number of agricultural products... [this] produced a great weakness in the [organization of] agriculture....

[There were] certain achievements in the industrial field during the first years but I should also mention the errors made. Fundamentally, these were caused by a lack of precise understanding of the technological and economic elements necessary in the new industries installed during those years.

But despite early setbacks, Fidel Castro's faith in the revolutionary path to development was not shaken. He spoke in September 1963, on the third anniversary of the formation of the Committees for the Defence of the Revolution:

> The path of the revolution, the path followed by Cuba, although it may be long and hard, is the only path that promises the people a secure future, a great and stable future.

And, in answer to taunts from abroad that Cuba was turning away from its industrialization plans, Fidel Castro went on:

> All the people, all the revolutionary [leaders] have gained experience. We see things much more clearly. Today we have a much clearer view of our possibilities and a much better idea of how to invest our resources. We know what sugar means for us as a source of foreign exchange....
>
> And here is a source of resources, not only to meet our needs, but to develop the whole economy, to develop our industry, based on the principle of the most rational use of our human resources, our economic resources...
>
> And thus, our way to industrialization, the path we must follow becomes much clearer to us. Because under these conditions some industries will have priority over others... like electric power... hydraulic works... and an extensive programme for factory construction.

Economic development became an important part of every speech made by Fidel Castro. He was tireless in trying to create a development consciousness, in encouraging the Cuban people to commit themselves to their country's advancement. In January 1965, on the sixth anniversary of the Cuban Revolution, he spoke of the necessity to look forwards:

> We are still mainly concerned with the future. If we should happen to refer to something done in the past it is purely by way of example, proof or encouragement. We must understand, above all else, that we still have much to do.

Despite very real successes in some areas of the economy there was no room for complacency:

> One must realise that all things are of a

23 Fidel Castro in the Sierra Maestra with peasant farmers. Along with young people they were to become the main beneficiaries of the Cuban Revolution because of their support for the Rebel Army.

different nature, and that therefore one cannot set the same goals since not all things require the same time or the same techniques.

Cuba was pressing on with the plan to remedy the past neglect of the countryside, which had resulted in the growth of Havana at the expense of every other area. New schools, new hospitals, new housing which previously would have gone to the capital, were now diverted to the countryside. Fidel Castro explained the policy to those most affected, the people of Havana:

> This economic deformity has shown us that we must follow the policy — not of depriving the people of Havana, since this would neither be just nor right — but of concentrating on the development of the rest of the country, on doing justice to the rest of the country.
>
> Were I saying this in the Province of Oriente, for example, the circumstances might lead some into the error that I was merely being demagogic. But I am saying this precisely here, at a meeting in the Capital of the country, and I am addressing the workers of the Capital. I am saying it precisely here because it is a matter of concern to the revolutionary working population of the Capital.
>
> Historically, these evils have not only been a detriment to the countryside, but also to all our workers including those of the Capital. As the resources of the nation and of every province in the country are developed, there will be a rise in the standard of living for all workers, wherever they may live. But the neglect of our villages and rural areas in the past was so great that today the only just and right policy is to spend the greatest effort on developing them.

He went on to explain how the young leaders of the Revolution did lose sight of their country's greatest resource:

> At the beginning of the Revolution we possibly failed to appreciate fully the exceptional natural conditions of the country and the possibilities in agriculture . . . . because of the need to develop

24 The old and the new. Prefabricated houses begin to replace the traditional "bohio" of the Cuban countryside, made of palms and palm thatch.

industry, we underestimated the possibilities in agriculture.

In industry one first requires machinery, installations of all kinds, technicians, and so on, whereas the most important element in agriculture, one might even say its capital, is the land; and this capital we already have, in the form of excellent land which can furthermore be used nearly all the year round.

No European country, no prosperous and industrialised country in the world has such a climate as Cuba. Neither in Europe, nor the United States, nor any other country, in the temperate zone, are there such possibilities for agriculture as in Cuba.

We have therefore realized that, under the new conditions where we have practically unlimited markets, where the needs of the country grow day by day and where there is a practically unlimited domestic market, agriculture must form the basis of our development; and the industrialisation of the country will not be postponed but will advance parallel to the progress in agriculture. Agriculture will therefore be the basis of the country's economic development and also the basis of its industrial development.

Nevertheless, Cuba could point to areas of *real* development in the first years of the Revolution, especially in health, employment and education, and this quickly became a matter of pride. In 1961 the US President, John F. Kennedy, established a development programme for Latin America, the Alliance for Progress, which would improve conditions in those countries in the same way as had happened in Cuba. The United States hoped thus to ensure that there would be no more revolutions like the Cuban one. But for Fidel Castro, there was no comparison with what was being achieved in Cuba, as he made clear to the Congress of Women of All America in January 1963:

In one of his speeches Mr. Kennedy said,

25 The battle for economic development: Che Guevara sets an example by driving a cane-cutting machine, March 1963.

"Let us compare Cuba with the Alliance for Progress". If we make the comparison, then Mr. Kennedy is lost. Because here, despite all the imperialist propaganda, it is a fact that every child is guaranteed a litre of milk daily. We had to establish rationing because employment increased considerably; nearly half a million people began to work, to have an income; the farmers stopped paying land rent; urban rents were lowered 50%; all education became free; hospital service increased five-fold; the people had incomparably greater means.

And logically, in those conditions we had to adopt measures which would guarantee all families the goods they need at a just price. Because a large enough number of rich people remained here to establish all sorts of speculation.

If it were a question of price, as happens in capitalist countries there they would

26 Fidel Castro helps move cement bags in an Oriente factory, August 1964. By their example, government leaders hoped to encourage all workers to give their best efforts to the economy.

27 May Day Parade 1965. The proximity of the USA and the experience at the Bay of Pigs and the October Missile Crisis the next year resulted in a military commitment out of proportion to Cuba's resources.

fix it with prices. They raise the price of milk to two pesos a litre, and then there is enough milk for those who have two pesos. They raise the price of rice to three pesos a pound, and then there is enough rice for those who have three pesos; they raise the price of beef to five pesos, and then there is enough for those who have five pesos. There is no rationing; there is something much worse. Everything goes to those who have, and nothing goes to those who have less. But they do try to sow confusion with all these things.

What Cuba was trying to achieve was quite different from the ideal of the USA:

> What you don't see in our country are new cars. You can go to Havana and you'll find lots of beat-up old cars. Anybody with a consumer society mentality who thinks that progress consists of neon signs and new cars can be perfectly certain that he will not understand Cuba. Whoever digs down deep enough among our people and sees the work the Revolution has done in the human sphere, will then understand our country.

The Export of Revolution?

Even in those early years of the Revolution, Cuba's links – and what was seen as its responsibility too – were clear with regard to other underdeveloped countries. On May Day 1966 Fidel Castro said:

> Our present duty as a poor underdeveloped country is to make the maximum effort to rid ourselves of poverty, misery and underdevelopment. But in the future we must not think of great affluence while other people still need our help. We must begin now to educate our children in the idea that tomorrow when all our pressing needs are supplied, our goal will be more than simply affluence. Our ideal is not wealth. Our firm ideal and our duty must be to help those peoples who were left behind.

He was to make the same points two years later when speaking to the Cuban people on television, analysing contemporary events in Czechoslovakia:

> Those who struggle for Communism in any country in the world can never forget the suffering, underdevelopment, poverty, ignorance, and exploitation that exist in a part of the world or how much poverty and destitution have accumulated there.
>
> When we give technical aid, we do not think of sending a bill to anyone, because we think that the least a developed country, a Socialist country, a revolutionary country, can do to help the underdeveloped world is to send technicians.
>
> And that is the way we act. Moreover, it is not a virtue. It is something elementary. And the day we have thousands or tens of thousands of technicians, the most elementary of our duties will be to contribute at least with technical aid for the countries which liberate themselves after us and which need our aid.

Latin America, to which Cuba was linked both historically and culturally, was seen as ripe for revolution. In September 1960 the First Declaration of Havana was published — a forceful statement of Cuba's foreign policy, of its links with Latin America, and a clear rejection of US claims to the area. It concludes with a clear commitment to work towards revolutionary change throughout the continent:

> The People of Cuba affirm [their] faith that Latin America, united and victorious will soon be free of the bonds that now make its economies rich spoils for the imperialism of North America; that keeps its true voice from being heard at conferences where cowed ministers form a solid chorus to the despotic masters. [We] confirm, therefore, [our] decision to work for this common Latin American destiny, which will allow our countries to build a true solidarity, founded in the free decision of each and the common goals of all.

The Declaration ends:

> We are ready! Cuba will not fail. Cuba is

28 From April 1961 Cuba was launched on a socialist path to development and a progressively closer economic and political relationship with the USSR. In the poster Fidel Castro is seen next to Karl Marx and Lenin.

here today to proclaim before Latin America and the world its historic and unchangeable resolution: Our country or death!

Funds, training and political support were provided for revolutionary groups active in most countries in Latin America, trying to repeat the experience of the 26th July Movement. Fidel Castro gave repeated encouragement and in February 1962 made the Second Declaration of Havana, after Cuba's expulsion from the OAS:

> The duty of every revolutionary is to make the revolution. It is known that the revolution will triumph in America and throughout the world but it is not for revolutionaries to sit in the doorways of their houses and wait for the corpse of imperialism to pass by. The role of Job does not suit a revolutionary.
>
> The wave of anger, of demands for justice, of claims for rights, which is beginning to sweep the lands of Latin America, will not stop. That wave will swell with every passing day. For that wave is composed of the greatest number, the majorities in every respect, those whose labour amasses the wealth and turns the wheels of history. Now they are awakening from the long, brutalising sleep to which they have been subjected. For this great humanity has said, "Enough!" and has begun to march. And their giant march will not be halted until they conquer true independence.

This speech of Fidel Castro's, only a tiny piece of which is reprinted here, was regarded as an important contribution to the revolutionary movement throughout the world and especially in Latin America. It was translated into all the most important languages and given the widest possible distribution. It was even miniaturized and printed on stamps in English, French and Spanish to be read with a magnifier. But Fidel's optimism, with regard to continent-wide revolution, was unfounded; in country after country, the revolution failed. And in Bolivia, Che Guevara, Fidel Castro's great friend and comrade-in-arms, was killed trying to foment revolution.

Che Guevara in Bolivia

> Che was an incomparable soldier and incomparable leader. From a military point of view, Che was extraordinarily courageous, extraordinarily aggressive. If, as a guerilla, he had his Achilles heel, it was this excessively aggressive quality, his absolute contempt for danger.
>
> His blood fell on our soil when he was wounded in several battles; and his blood was shed in Bolivia for the redemption of the exploited and the oppressed. That blood was shed for the sake of all the exploited and all the oppressed.

This is how Fidel Castro described Che Guevara, killed in battle in Bolivia, to thousands of Cubans who had come to hear the eulogy on 18 October 1967.

Before leaving Cuba in 1965, to begin the revolution elsewhere, Che had renounced his government position and freed Cuba from all responsibilities for his actions. In a letter to Fidel Castro in April 1965 he wrote:

> Other lands of the world demand the contribution of my modest efforts. I can do what is denied to you, on account of your responsibility as Cuba's leader — and the hour of parting has come.
>
> I free Cuba from all responsibility except that which derives from its example. And if my final hour should come under other skies, my last thought will be for this people, and especially for you. That I thank you for what you have taught me and for your examples, and that I will be true to my beliefs.
>
> Wherever I go I will feel the responsibility of being a Cuban Revolutionary and will act accordingly.
>
> It is much easier to win a revolutionary war than it is to develop a country and build socialism.

The last comment, no doubt, referred to Fidel Castro remaining in Cuba to fight the battle for Cuba's development.

Disguised as a businessman, with his beard shaved off, travelling by a circuitous route, Che arrived in Bolivia, where he set up his guerilla base.

Rumour circulated throughout the world: Che had been killed in the Dominican Republic; he was fighting in the Congo, in Venezuela, in Viet Nam, in Laos; even that Fidel Castro had had him killed.

Then, in April 1967, Che sent a message to the Tricontinental Conference in Havana:

> The time has come to settle our disagreements [about the best way to make the revolution] and place everything we have at the service of the struggle. This means a long war. And a cruel war . . . . Whenever death may surprise us it will be welcome, provided that this, our battle cry, reaches some receptive ears, that another hand be extended to take up our weapons.

When the US government heard rumours of Che's presence in Bolivia, highly trained troops were sent to bolster up the Bolivian army. Sophisticated equipment, including satellite tracking, was used to locate Che, and his Cuban and Bolivian companions.

On 8 October 1967 Bolivian Rangers, led by US advisers, caught up with a group of guerillas in the mountains. Their leader was caught and taken to a village nearby, where he was put in the local school. It was Che Guevara. He was beaten, questioned and the next day shot. His body was then taken to the nearby town of Vallegrande, where it was put on show to the local people and journalists, to be finally cremated and scattered at an unknown spot somewhere in Bolivia.

When the news of Che's death reached Cuba, Fidel Castro spoke for all Cubans when he said:

> Such an example can never be wiped out by anything or anyone.
>
> If we wish to express what we want

29 Che Guevara in the Sierra Maestra.

the men of future generations to be like, we must say: Let them be like Che! If we wish to express what we want our children to be like, we must say from our hearts, We want them to be like Che!

The New Man

Che was seen as one of the best examples of the Cuban Revolution. He had selflessly sacrificed himself, firstly through his work, then by giving his life. His idea of the "New Man" — a man of a truly "Communist consciousness" — who could be formed by the right education, was carried on after his death. Forming the "New Man" was seen as the great task of the Revolution.

Che had explained how the New Man and New Woman, would be formed:

> Youth . . . is particularly important because it is the malleable clay with which the new man, without previous defects, can be formed. The youth receives treatment

that matches our ambitions. In education, study and work are combined from the very beginning. Students do manual work during the vacation or together with their studies. In some cases work is a prize, while in others it's an educational tool; it is never a punishment. A new generation is being born.

It was in the economy of Cuba that these ideas found their greatest expression. Man would be motivated by the needs of society, not by his own ambitions. Man did not work for money, nor for consumer goods; in fact, money would increasingly lose its former role. Fidel Castro explained the concept to a group of workers in December 1967:

> Through work we will create material wealth; through your work we will create human awareness. We will bring up human beings devoid of selfishness, devoid of defects of the past, human beings with a collective sense of effort, a collective sense of strength.

Che was constantly evoked as the example to be followed.

Fidel Castro explained what it was hoped could be achieved, in his anniversary speech on 26 July 1968:

> We should not use money or wealth to create political awareness. We must use political awareness to create wealth. To offer a man more to do more is to buy his conscience with money. To give a man participation in more collective wealth because he does his duty and produces more and creates more for society is to turn political awareness into wealth.
>
> Of course the Revolution was unable to give the people all that they needed; the people could not be given what the Revolution did not have to give. But the Revolution has sought to give the people all that it had to give.
>
> But we will never create a socialist consciousness with "dollar sign" in the minds and hearts of our men and women.

In 1968 private shops and businesses were closed down in what came to be known as "The Revolutionary Offensive". Fidel Castro explained this in a long and detailed speech at the University of Havana on 13 March, on the eleventh anniversary of the attack on the Presidential Palace:

> We did not make a Revolution here to establish the right to trade! When will they finally understand that this is a Revolution of socialists, of Communists. When will they learn that nobody shed his blood here fighting against the tyranny, against mercenaries, against bandits, in order to establish the right for someone to make two hundred pesos selling rum, or fifty pesos selling fried eggs, or omelettes, while the secretaries who work in State enterprises earn modest incomes, the modest incomes that the present development of our country's economy allows?
>
> We cannot encourage or even permit selfish attitudes among men if we don't want men to be guided by the instinct of selfishness, of individuality; by the wolf, the beast instinct; man as the enemy of man, the exploiter of man, the setter of snares for other men.
>
> We don't feel that the Communist man can be developed by encouraging man's ambition, man's individual desires. If we are going to fail because we believe in man's ability, in his ability to improve, then we will fail, but we will never renounce our faith in mankind.
>
> We have known many cases of men acting from a sense of honour, giving something more than their work; driven by profoundly moral factors.
>
> Can an underdeveloped country do anything else?

The most important "moral" task set by Fidel Castro was to achieve a sugar harvest of 10 million tons in 1970, which was to wipe out some of Cuba's indebtedness to the Soviet Union and to pay for the next phase of Cuba's development.

Chapter Five

The Battle for the Ten Millions and the Institutionalization of the Cuban Revolution

The Battle for the 10 Million Tons

In the Soviet Union in January 1964 Fidel Castro announced that Cuba would achieve a sugar harvest of 10 million tons in 1970. On television, on 20 May 1970, he explained to the Cuban people how this ambitious goal had come about:

> Ever since we opened trade relations with the Soviet Union, following the aggression of the United States of America which deprived us of our sugar quota, the USSR purchased the sugar which had been shut out of the United States of America's market. The first sugar it purchased was paid for at more or less the going price on the international market.
>
> As you know, part of our sugar is sold on what is known as the free market, and another is sold through trade agreements with different countries. Sugar prices are subject to fluctuation but usually the prices stipulated in the trade agreements are higher than those of the free market.
>
> Our country needed oil, a whole series of raw materials, food stuffs and equipment, and there was no place to get them from other than the USSR.
>
> As a result, our imports from the USSR grew considerably, while our paying ability was limited. The amount of sugar we could sell was limited, as also were some other products we sold it following the United States of America's blockade.
>
> Sugar was the most important of our exports followed by minerals, small amounts of tobacco, etc.
>
> As a result of conditions created by the yankee blockade, it was very difficult for us to make purchases in other markets. We experienced not only foreign exchange difficulties, but practical difficulties even when we had foreign exchange.
>
> We began purchasing a great number of items that were necessary for our economy from the socialist camp — especially from the Soviet Union.
>
> As a result of this and the needs of a developing country — we might even say of a disorganised country, as every country in the first stage of a revolutionary process is disorganised — our trade deficit with the USSR grew with every passing year.
>
> This was the reason, the need, for making a great plan for increasing our sugar exports. It was not the result of a whim or the desire to set ourselves difficult goals or obtain glory by producing 10 million tons of sugar; rather, it was the result of a real need. And, also, it was the only possibility our country had, the only way through which — by taking full advantage of the land, increased productivity per unit area, making full use of existing capacity, lengthening the harvest period and installing some new equipment — we could obtain a

400 million peso increase in our exports.

Cuba had never produced 10 million tons of sugar before. The largest harvest so far achieved had been in 1961, just after the beginning of the Revolution, when 6¾ million tons of sugar had been produced. But, as Fidel Castro explained, Cuba had, in sugar, the possibilities of expanding production and of deriving considerable benefits from the increase in exports.

Cuba's economic development has not been linked solely with the other socialist countries, like the Soviet Union, but has always relied for part of its technological needs on the West — hence the need for hard currency.

When the harvest began on 14 July 1969, Fidel Castro indicated how important it was politically, as well as economically:

> This sugar harvest begins today and will not end until the last sack of sugar for the 10 million tons has been produced. We will demonstrate to the world what a revolutionary people can do. This example will go down in history.

The whole country was motivated for the 10 million tons. Posters everywhere exhorted Cubans to make whatever contribution they could during holidays and at weekends. Thousands of soldiers were moved into the country to cut cane, young volunteers from the USA, the "Venceremos Brigades", went to Cuba to help in the effort. It was very different from pre-Revolutionary times when people had been forced to work, in dreadful conditions, just in order to survive. Now the cane-cutter had a very different place in society, as Fidel Castro made clear to the workers who gathered to celebrate May Day in 1966 in Revolution Square, Havana:

> The sweat of the men and women of this country will never again serve the privileged or the exploiters. But it is not true that because of this, as a result of the revolution, we shall have fewer millionaires in this country. Now, we have more millionaires!

30 Fidel Castro and the other government leaders took their turn at cutting cane during the Battle for the 10 Million Tons.

> But they are not millionaires in the old sense . . . .
>
> Our millionaires of today are not those who exploit the work of others, but those who by their own work are capable of cutting a million *arrobas* of sugar cane. They are not millionaires whose fortune is gained at the expense of others; but millionaires by their own work.
>
> In the past the millionaires were different. There were only a few, and they did not cut cane or shed a drop of sweat. The millionaires were precisely those who did not work but made others work for them.

Just as he had done during the Literacy Campaign in 1961, Fidel Castro gave television reports on the progress of the harvest: problems of drought here, machinery breakdown there, not enough people here, cane-cutting machine operating successfully there. The "Zafra" (sugar harvest) was on everybody's lips.

But despite all efforts, the 10 million tons target was not reached. The first clues to why were in the problems being experienced in different parts of the country; machinery breakdowns, problems with transportation, low cane yields and bad weather over which nobody, not even Fidel Castro, had control. In April 1970, at a public rally to welcome fishermen back to Cuba, who had been kidnapped, Fidel Castro admitted that the 10 million tons would not be produced.

To the Cubans listening to him, with tears rolling down their cheeks, Fidel Castro could only offer this comfort:

> We have gone all out, working towards this goal, we have devoted every last atom of our energy, of our thought and our feelings towards it. And the only thing I have left to say to any Cuban — to those who are most deeply wounded in their souls, who are most deeply grieved by this news — is that we feel the same grief as they do; it is the same grief, I feel now. And I want those whose pride and revolutionary honour has been most deeply wounded to know I feel the same stab to my dignity, pride and honour.

On 26 July 1970, the Moncada anniversary, Fidel Castro openly admitted the problems caused by the failure of the 10 million tons attempt in a speech known as the "Autocritica":

> Our enemies say we have problems, and in this our enemies are right. They say there is discontent, and in reality our enemies are right. They say there is irritation and in reality our enemies are right. As you see, we are not afraid to admit when our enemies are right.
>
> We are going to begin in the first place, by pointing out the responsibility which all of us, and I in particular, have for these problems. I am in no way trying to pin the blame on anyone not in the revolutionary leadership and myself. Unfortunately this self-criticism cannot be accompanied by other logical solutions. It would be better to tell the people to look for someone else. (Shouts "No".) It would be

31 Cane-cutting machinery has not been easy to apply in Cuba because of the undulating ground. By 1980, however, 50 per cent of sugar cane was cut by this method.

better, but it would be hypocritical on our part.

I believe that we, the leaders of the Revolution, have cost the people too much in our process of learning. And unfortunately our problem, one of our most difficult problems — and we are paying for it dearly — is our heritage of ignorance.

When we spoke of illiterates we didn't include ourselves among the illiterates or even among the semi-illiterates! We could best be classified as ignorant. And we were ignorant — almost without exception (and I, of course, am not the exception) — all of us. The problem is even worse. Signs of illiteracy or semi-literacy can be found in many men in positions of responsibility.

We began as revolutionaries not in a factory, which would have been a great help to us all. We began as revolutionaries through the study of theory, the intellectual road, the road of thought. And it would have helped all of us if we had come from the factories and known more about them, because it is there that the really revolutionary spirit of which Marx and Lenin spoke is to be found.

There was no doubt that the failure of the 10 million tons harvest did represent an enormous setback to the Revolution. But Fidel Castro considered that the lesson could be put to good advantage. In his speech to the Cuban fishermen in April, he had said:

> The Revolution has suffered setbacks — real setbacks — on more than one occasion. How many times did we suffer setbacks in the course of our revolutionary history? In the Moncada attack; after the *Granma* landing when there were only six or seven of us left, with only a few rifles; at the time of the April 1958 strike . . . many, many times.
>
> A revolutionary people learns from its victories, but it learns even more from its setbacks.
>
> We should have a revolutionary fortitude to convert this setback into a victory.

From then on, huge posters were to be seen throughout Cuba. On an orange background, the word "REVES" (the Spanish for "setback") appears in the bottom quarter, with a huge V for Victory emerging from the letter V.

But the failure had caused enormous problems to the entire economy, with everything other than sugar dislocated in the attempt. Re-evaluation and changes were necessary.

A Change of Direction?

The setback of the 10 million tons had repercussions throughout Cuban society and the economy, and even in the role of Fidel Castro himself. In the economy, less importance was given now to moral incentives; and instead material incentives — bonuses, wage differentials and more consumer goods — were introduced. In a speech on the Moncada anniversary in 1973 (the most important policy speeches are often made on this date) Fidel Castro described moral incentives as "idealistic errors [which] we must bravely correct in the way of handling the economy". Whereas hitherto, Cuba was seen as developing Communism and socialism at the same time, now there was no doubt about its state of development:

> We are in the socialist stage of the Revolution, in which, due to the material realities and the level of culture and awareness in a society that has just emerged from capitalist society, the form of distribution that corresponds is the one outlined by Karl Marx [in the *Critique of the Gotha Programme*], from each according to his capacity, to each according to his work.

On the other hand, moral incentives would not be completely displaced:

> It is true that many of our workers are real examples of Communists. They are the vanguard of what all society will one day be like. But if we think and act as if that was the conduct of every member of society, we would be guilty of idealism and

32 Until the "Institutionalization" of the Revolution in the 1970s the long informative speeches made by Fidel Castro were the main vehicle of communication between the government and the people.

33 Raul Castro, Fidel's younger brother and designated successor, who participated in the attack on the Moncada and was a combatant in the Sierra Maestra.

34 The CDRs (Committees for the Defence of the Revolution), one of which is seen here in 1975 welcoming Fidel Castro, are an important political as well as social organization.

the result would be that the greatest share of the social load would unjustly fall on the best, without any moral results in the awareness of the most backward, and it would have equally negative effects on the economy. Together with moral incentives, we must have material incentives, without abusing either one, because the former would lead us to idealism, while the latter would lead to individual selfishness.
We must act in such a way that economic incentives will not become the exclusive motivation of man, nor moral incentives serve to have some live off the work of the rest.

In addition to individual rewards for workers who produced more than their norm, resources were also provided for their communities, to build clinics, schools and housing. Cuban trade unions, for which Che Guevara saw little role in a socialist society, agreed to these dramatic changes.

A new enhanced role was decided upon for all the mass organizations, as well as for the trade unions: for example, for the Committees for the Defence of the Revolution (CDRs), community-based organizations, responsible for a wide range of social services; for the Cuban Federation of Women (FMC); and for political organizations, the Cuban Communist Party (PCC) and the Young Communist League.

Fidel Castro's position, too, changed. Throughout the 1960s, with a group of trusted men and women around him, many of them "Moncadistas", he had wielded enormous power. For that reason, he has been dubbed a "dictator", although those close to him say that this image is quite wrong.

After 1959 in Cuba there were few political institutions, such as a government or constitution, because Batista had destroyed them.

And the Revolutionary government, led by Fidel Castro, was in no hurry to introduce others. It governed by decree. Che Guevara explained in 1965:

> We are seeking something new that will allow a perfect identification between the government and the community as a whole. Some experiments have been carried out with the aim of gradually creating the institutionalization of the Revolution *but without too much hurry*. We have been greatly restrained by the fear that any formal aspect might make us lose sight of the ultimate and most revolutionary aspiration: to see men freed from alienation.
> (from *Man and Socialism in Cuba*)

The 1970s can be seen as the period of the Institutionalization of the Cuban Revolution — when decision-making was decentralized and power began to be put back in the hands of the people. During this time membership of the Communist Party was increased, a new Socialist Constitution was introduced, elections began, a "Family Code" was introduced, giving rights and responsibilities to the family, and Cuba's first Five Year Plan for economic development was started. Many observers see the 10 million tons setback as provoking all this, though the Cuban view is the reverse: the time was not right for Institutionalization until the 1970s. Until then the provisional government was having to defend the Revolution from inside and outside attacks, and then supervise the economic struggle for the giant sugar harvest.

One of the first steps in the Institutionalization of the Revolution was to increase the membership of the Cuban Communist Party (PCC). Fidel Castro spoke of the role of the Party in his 26 July speech in 1975:

> Like the Cuban Revolutionary Party [formed by José Martí] at the time of Independence, our Party today is leading the Revolution. Membership in it, far from being a source of privilege, demands sacrifices and total dedication to the revolutionary cause. In the uncertain times of the 26th July [1953] and in the early years of the Revolution, individuals played a decisive role, a role now carried out by the Party. Men die, but the Party is immortal.
>
> The political apparatus must be strengthened. The Party does not administer, it guides, directs, supports and guarantees the fulfilment of the plans of the revolutionary leadership in every area.

In December 1975, for the first time in its revolutionary history, the Cuban Communist Party held a Congress, at which Fidel Castro, as the First Secretary, gave a ten-hour report. He pointed out the importance of the event:

> The First Congress has enormous historical importance. After the first Congress we shall enter a new stage of the Revolution, with a more advanced level of work on the part of the mass organisations and Party, with much more evolved political awareness and with more profound analysis of all our activities.

The involvement of the Cuban people in decision-making took a real step forward with the start of *Poder Popular* (People's Power), which was introduced for a year's trial, in Matanzas Province in 1974. Elections were held for delegates to a Municipal Assembly. In his Moncada anniversary speech that year Fidel Castro said:

> These were elections of the revolutionary people, organised by the revolutionary people, and for the service of the revolutionary people. . . .
>
> The recent elections in Matanzas have been the cleanest in the history of our country: elections without backroom dealing, without fraud, without demagogy, without politicking. No one had to hope for anything, because it wasn't personal ambitions that determined the nomination of the candidate, but collective aspirations. And without election campaigns because the campaign here is the everyday life of the candidate nominated by the people;

his campaign is his own life story, his conduct through the years, his record of service to his country.

In 1976 the system tried out in Matanzas was applied to the whole of Cuba.

Delegates are directly elected to sit on Municipal Assemblies, being responsible for a wide range of services in their area. Above the Municipal Assemblies are the Provincial Assemblies, and above them the National Assembly of People's Power (NAPP) situated in Havana. Elections to the Provincial Assemblies and National Assembly are indirect. The NAPP elects the Council of State, whose President is the Head of Government and of State. In 1976 Fidel Castro was elected the first President.

To draw together all the administrative changes, a new, socialist Constitution was drawn up to replace the old pre-Revolutionary Constitution. It was first discussed by everyone and amended considerably, before being put before the people again in a referendum in February 1976. Ninety per cent of the adult population voted in a secret ballot, with young students on duty at the ballot-boxes. Ninety-seven per cent were in favour.

35 "Biographies" of all the candidates for People's Power, containing their faults as well as strengths, are given wide publicity during elections. In this cartoon, which appeared in 1976, the man is surprised to find, on seeing the poster, that the candidate called José Perez is in fact a man he knows called Pépé.

Chapter Six

The Revolution Becomes Respectable?

Coming Out of the Cold

The internal changes in Cuba were matched by a revolution in the country's relations with the rest of the world. Diplomatic relations were established with Latin American countries — firstly with the Chilean government, led by Salvador Allende, in 1970, to be followed by others ignoring the pressures of the Organization of American States (OAS), led by the USA. The effects were felt in Cuba economically as well as diplomatically, for goods previously kept out of the country were now allowed in, and Cuba could begin to trade again with the Latin American nations, with which it had always identified. Fidel Castro spoke in 1974 of Cuba's position

> Cuba belongs to Latin America, historically, morally and culturally. We feel that we are a part of Latin America. Some day our natural and cultural ties with the peoples of the rest of Latin America will reach full development. Some day we will belong to an association, an organisation: but this would have to be the association or organisation of revolutionary states of Latin America.

The USA's blockade still remained, but in 1974 Fidel Castro was optimistic that it could not last much longer and that relations with the USA would improve. At the start of the 1980s, and with a new US President, the blockade still existed, but relations had altered.

The USA and Cuba

There is little doubt that, while it has hindered the progress and development of the Cuban Revolution, the offensive launched by the US government against Cuba has also aided the Revolutionaries by uniting them against a common enemy. Castro told an American journalist in 1979:

> We cannot forget that against our people's will the United States of America has occupied a piece of our territory; the United States of America has troops and warships at the Guantánamo naval base.
>
> This is a situation that has gone on for 20 years and needless to say, five administrations have been in the White House. All the plans against the Revolution have failed. Cuba is not more isolated; Cuba is less isolated than ever. The prestige of the Cuban Revolution is not smaller; it is greater than ever before.

Being so close to the USA — 145 kilometres away at the nearest point, Cuba would gain considerably by the re-establishment of diplomatic and, more importantly, perhaps, economic relations. Fidel Castro has always made clear that Cuba's quarrel is not with the

36 Fidel Castro greeted enthusiastically during his visit to Chile in 1971.

people of the USA; but with the government:

... we do not preach hatred towards the people of the United States of America. On the contrary, we have always seen with sympathy the development of an awareness among the people of the United States of America itself, the development of the struggle of the people of the United States of America, the anti-war demonstrations, and the struggles for civil rights. We make a clear distinction between the people of the United States of America and imperialist government.

The crucial question has always been the blockade. At the second session of the NAPP in 1977 Fidel Castro said:

We have nothing to negotiate with the imperialist government of the United States of America. Debts to the imperialist government? Mines, Cuban lands, banks, natural resources and trade rights which were recovered by the Cuban people? Such property cannot be paid for. No question about it! We will never pay one single penny, not even one single token penny to the imperialists who exploited us, who made millions at the expense of our sweat and our blood.

It is not we who are indebted to them. It is they who are indebted to us, for the vast material and human damage they have inflicted on us as a result of their blockade, enormous aggression and repeated political and military outrages.

During the Presidency of Gerald Ford (1974-77) moves did get underway towards a re-establishment of relations. (There was no chance of such moves while Richard Nixon was President (1968-74), as he had been the least sympathetic of all US Presidents towards Cuba.) Diplomats were exchanged and "Interest Sections" of each country were established in Havana and Washington respectively. Cultural exchanges of sportsmen, musicians and ballet dancers began. It became legal once more for US philatelists to obtain Cuban stamps, and tourism to Cuba was re-established. But relations cooled again with the news of Cuba's involvement in Africa. At the Second Session of the NAPP Fidel Castro responded angrily:

> What moral basis can the United States of America have to speak about the Cuban troops in Africa? What moral basis can a country have whose troops are on every continent? What moral basis can the United States of America have to speak about our troops in Africa when their own troops are stationed right here in our own national territory at the Guantánamo naval base?

The moral position of the USA became less strong with the public admission that the US government had repeatedly tried to kill or discredit Fidel Castro and members of the Cuban government.

Assassination Attempts on the Life of Fidel Castro

On 6 October 1976 a civilian DC8 airliner belonging to Cubana, Cuba's national airline, was sabotaged and crashed into the sea off Barbados with the loss of all seventy-three people on board. Fidel Castro was not aboard the plane, but he linked this outrage to others perpetrated by the CIA against himself and other government leaders, when he spoke to over a million Cuban people who had gathered in honour of those killed:

> I wish to recall that the CIA has been the instigator of criminal methods that have increasingly affected the international community in recent years. The CIA plotted and encouraged skyjacking in order to use it against Cuba during the early years of the Revolution; the CIA plotted pirate attacks from foreign bases in its aggressive policy against Cuba; the CIA plotted the destabilisation of foreign governments; the CIA revived for modern times the deplorable policy of plotting and committing assassinations of leaders of other countries; the CIA has now plotted the ominous scheme to blow up civilian airplanes in flight. The world community must be aware of the gravity of these events.
>
> We suspect that the United States government has not given up such practices. On October 9, only three days after the criminal sabotage in Barbados, a message sent by the CIA to an agent in Havana, was intercepted. That message, transmitted from the CIA's central headquarters in Langley, Virginia, says in part: "Please inform at earliest opportunity any data concerning Fidel's attendance at the ceremony for the first anniversary of Angola's independence, November 11. If he's going, try to get complete itinerary for Fidel's

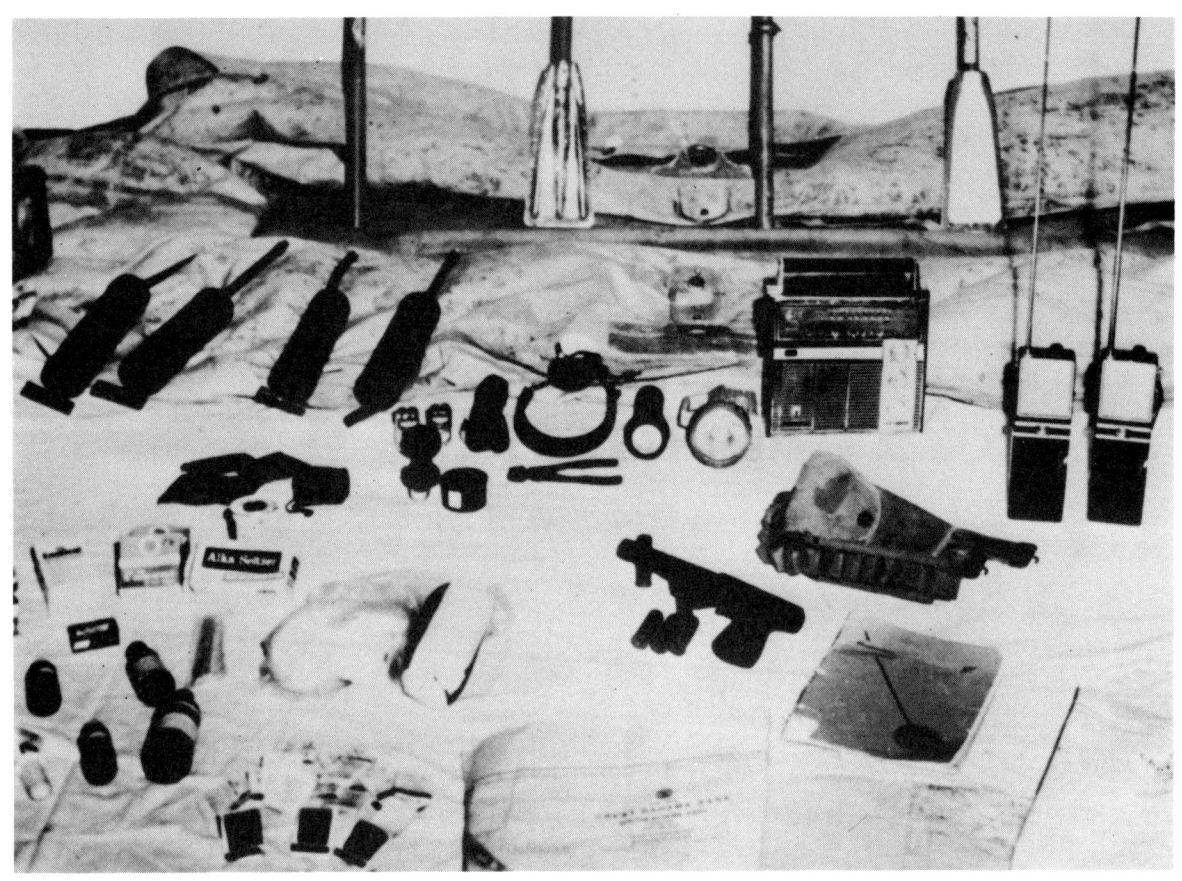

37 Equipment belonging to the CIA discovered in Cuba.

visit to other countries on the same trip.

There have been many attempts to kill Fidel Castro. The American government's responsibility for them came to be publicly admitted during the Watergate Affair in the USA, which led to the disgrace and resignation of President Nixon in 1974. Details of some of the plots were published in 1975 by the United States Senate Sub-Committee, presided over by Senator Church:

> We have found concrete evidence of at least eight plots involving the CIA to assassinate Fidel Castro from 1960 to 1965. Although some of the assassination plots did not advance beyond the stage of planning and preparation, one plot, involving the participation of underworld figures, twice progressed to the point of sending poison pills to Cuba and dispatching teams to commit the act. Another plot involved furnishing weapons and other assassination devices to a Cuban dissident.
>
> From March through August 1960, during the last year of the Eisenhower Administration, the CIA considered plans to undermine Castro's charismatic appeal by sabotaging his speeches; a scheme was discussed to spray Castro's broadcasting studio with a chemical which produced similar effects to LSD, but the scheme was unreliable. During this period, Technical Services Division (TSD) [of the CIA] impregnated a box of cigars with a chemical which produced temporary disorientation hoping to induce Castro to smoke one of the cigars before delivering a speech. [Another plan] was to destroy Castro's image as "The Beard" by dusting his shoes with thallium salts, a strong depilatory that would cause his beard to fall out, to

be administered during a trip outside Cuba. The chemical was tested on animals but abandoned as a scheme because Castro cancelled his trip.

Exploding seashells were developed to kill Castro when scuba diving, as well as more conventional assassination techniques, such as poisoning his cigars.

The Mafia, who had lost hotels and gambling facilities as well as income from prostitution and drugs in Cuba, because of the Revolution, were enlisted to help the CIA. Money was no object to the CIA. One Mafia contact was provided with a boat, radar equipment, radios and weapons with which to kill Castro and was never seen or heard of again. $ 50,000 were provided for one agent in Cuba if he was successful.

Fidel Castro was well aware of these attempts on his life and his "fatness" at some events could have been caused by a bullet-proof vest, though he publicly showed that he was not wearing one when he visited United Nations Headquarters in New York in 1979.

Cuba and The Third World

Cuba's relationship with the Third World, and with liberation groups in particular, has been a consistent strand of its foreign policy. Assistance to Third World countries and to liberation groups has taken many forms: for example, weapons were sent in the past to African and Latin American countries; and at other times men. More recently Cuba has sent doctors, nurses, teachers and construction workers to many countries in the Caribbean, Africa and Asia. At the Summit Conference of the Movement of Non-Aligned Countries in Havana in 1979, Fidel Castro gave an idea of Cuba's commitment:

> In our international relations we express solidarity with deeds, not fine words. Cuban technicians are now [in 1979] working in 28 countries of the [Non-Aligned] Movement.

The kind of assistance offered by Cuba can be seen in this description of its aid to Jamaica, summed up in 1977 by the Conference of

38 Fidel Castro as Chairman of the Movement of Non-Aligned Countries, addresses the United Nations, October 1979.

Caribbean Churches, representing all the different church groups in that region:

> Cuba has provided Jamaica with a wide range of assistance in educational, agricultural, health, trade, and other sectors. They constructed a series of micro-irrigation dams; built the most modern secondary school the country owns — at a cost of $4 million to educate 500 students with accommodation for boarding; established a pre-fab housing plant to produce building materials for a new township; trained more than 160 Jamaican youths in building construction in Cuba, where an additional 250 are being trained in the same field; provided scholarships in deep-sea fishing, language studies, and sports as well as making available 14 doctors to improve the efficiency of the Jamaican health service.

In the Caribbean, Guyana and Grenada, as well as Jamaica, have received this kind of assistance.

As Forbes Burnham, the Prime Minister of Guyana, said on a visit to Cuba, strong links unite Cuba with the other countries of the Caribbean:

> The historical and ethnical origins of our people are fairly close . . . we resemble each other in all aspects: we were all exploited by the monopolies; we all had to grow much cane and produce much sugar to enrich the foreign exploiters, we all had to work very hard to extract our natural resources for the benefit of the foreign exploiters; we all received the same legacy of underdeveloped culture, illiteracy, unemployment, lack of medical assistance and lack of the most essential means of subsistence; and now we all face the same task of developing our countries.

Michael Manley, former Prime Minister of Jamaica, spoke similarly of his country's links with Cuba, when Fidel Castro visited Jamaica in 1977. He described the nature of the aid provided by Cuba:

> They [the Cubans] want to share the technology of minidams — which we are working on now — so that another part of the world can benefit from irrigation. And wherever there are progressive processes in the world short of medicine, there you will find a Cuban doctor. And we find that never do they ask a favour in return, never do they attach strings.

The year before, in Cuba, Manley had said:

> Recently [in 1975] we had floods, caused by rains that did a lot of damage. We received many messages of sympathy from around the world and we received a little help from here and there. From Cuba there came an entire ship loaded to the very brim with articles to help our people.
>
> We, like you, 16 years ago, suffer from many desperate shortages of skills, know-how, of technology. And there are countries in the world that offered assistance but we found none that responds with action after words so rapidly as the Cuba of Fidel Castro.
>
> There is a saying in English, "By their deeds ye shall know them". By your deeds we are beginning to know you.

The US government, which has always looked upon the Caribbean as its own "backyard", showed great concern at the links Cuba was establishing in the region. In the 1980 elections in Jamaica the US supported Michael Manley's opponent, Edward Seaga, who, on gaining power, expelled the Cuban Ambassador from Jamaica and, although maintaining diplomatic relations with Cuba, curtailed most of the Cuban aid projects.

The new President of the USA, Ronald Reagan, saw the Jamaican elections as a "setback to Communism" in the Caribbean and quickly set about a harsher policy towards Cuba in 1981. Cuba was identified, by President Reagan and his government, as the source of all unrest in the Caribbean, as well as in Africa. They accused Cuba, for example, of "intervention" in El Salvador, where a fifty-year old struggle between the people and a succession of brutal governments appeared close to victory for the people, putting US interests in El Salvador in question. At the same time the US government was providing millions of dollars worth of arms to the government. Cuba was threatened by "military blockade", in addition to the economic blockade that already exists, and there were even threats to "mine the coast of Cuba". On the eve of the 20th Anniversary of the Bay of Pigs the Cuban government, incredulous, as Raul Castro put it, "that a government can fall over the same stone twice", expressed fears of a repeat invasion of Cuba, or Grenada or Nicaragua which were similarly making their own revolutions in the Caribbean.

But it was Cuba's relations further away in Africa which most concerned the US government in the 1970s. This was after Cuba had provided the Angolan government with military assistance in 1975. Fidel Castro explained Cuba's position in a speech on the 15th Anniversary of the Bay of Pigs invasion the following year:

> The people of Cuba sent their first instructors to Angola in October [1975]. South African officers, CIA agents, white mercenaries and troops from puppet governments had been in action in Angola for many months already, but Cuba had not sent a single military unit.
>
> On October 23rd, South African troops supported by artillery and tanks, invaded the Republic of Angola from the Namibian border. The mercenaries, meanwhile, were attacking from the North and were only 25 kilometres from Luanda [Angola's capital]. In view of this treacherous attack, on November 5th the Revolutionary Government of Cuba decided to send the first military units to Angola to support the MPLA.
>
> We Cubans helped our Angolan brothers and sisters, first and foremost on principle, because we are internationalists, and, secondly, because our people is both a Latin-American people and a Latin-African people. Millions of Africans were shipped to Cuba as slaves by the colonialists and a good part of Cuban blood is African blood.

To those who accused Cuba of being led by the Soviet Union, and not having a foreign policy of their own, Fidel Castro had this to say in the same speech:

> Cuba made its decision completely on its own responsibility. The Soviet Union — which had always helped the people of the Portuguese colonies in the struggle for their independence and provided besieged Angola with basic aid in military equipment and collaborated with our efforts when imperialism had cut off practically all our air routes to Africa — never requested that a single Cuban be sent to that country. The USSR is extraordinarily respectful and careful in its relations with Cuba. A decision of that nature could only be taken by our own Party.

He explained why Cuba is providing aid to Africa in his long interview with Barbara Walters in 1977 for American television:

> Africa is terribly backward; sanitary conditions are horrendous; there are countries that only have one doctor for every 100,000 people. Many countries have no universities or very few students; there are no technicians. The state of education and sanitation is terrible.

In Africa, he said, a different kind of development, a different kind of society, was necessary:

> Those countries can't follow the way of life of France, of Paris, of London, of New York or the United States of America. You [in the US] have created a certain way of life and a society that has great wealth, badly distributed of course, but you do possess great wealth.
>
> Do you think that the "American Way of Life" is the model for Africa, for India,

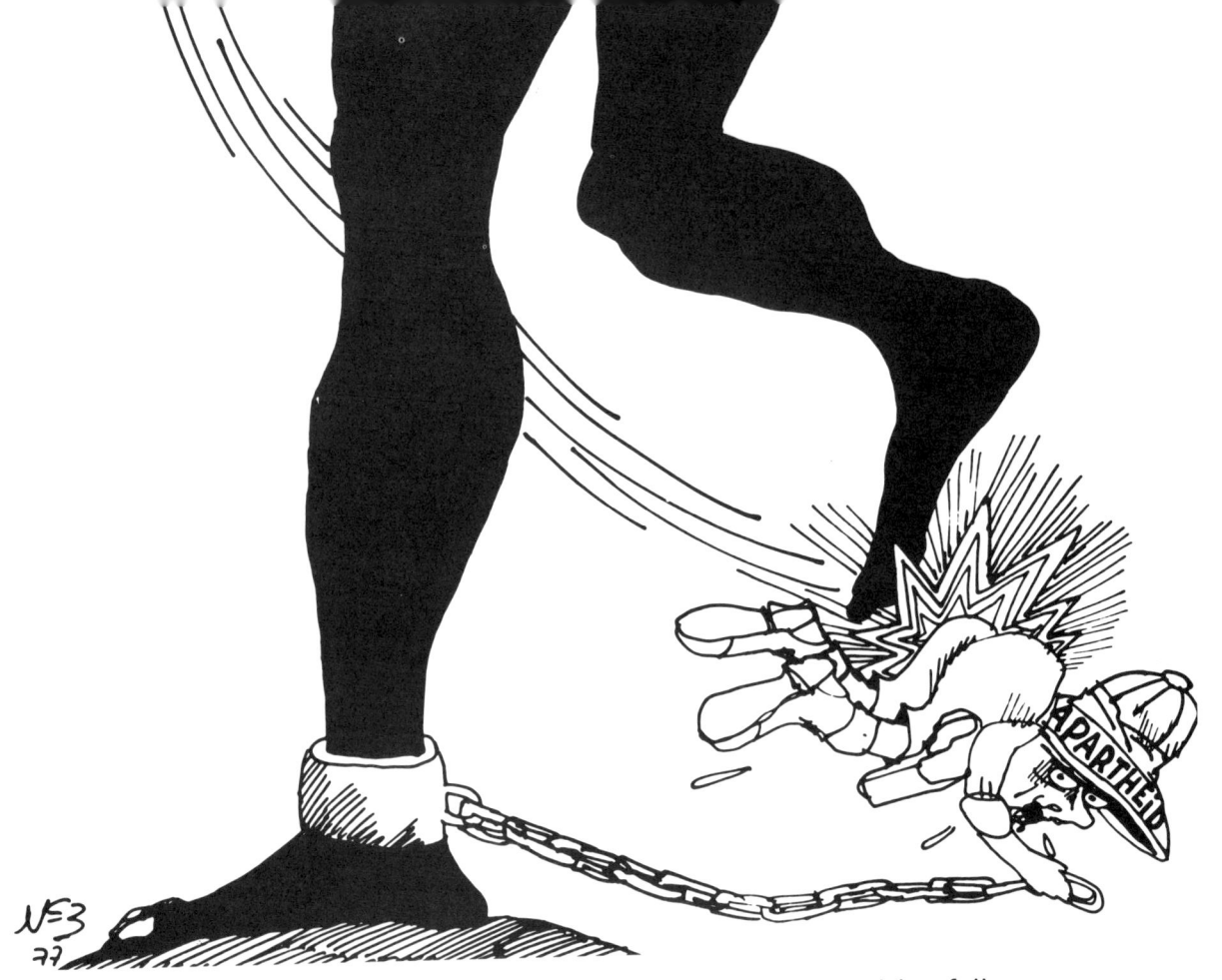

39 This cartoon by Nuez sums up Cuba's position with regard to apartheid in South Africa. Cuban support for African liberation has been a consistent part of its foreign policy.

for China? Just imagine what the situation would be like if every Chinese had a car; if every Indian had a car? How many years would the world oil reserves last? How long? You have created a society that is very good for you, but it is not the answer, and cannot be the model for the underdeveloped countries of the world, of Latin America, Asia, Africa. That is the reality.

Fidel Castro has many times denied that Cuba represents a "model" for development in the Third World. But, inevitably — because Cuba has given aid to less-developed countries than itself, and because it has shown the way forward in solving its own pressing economic and social problems — other countries are turning to it as a model to follow.

Fidel Castro's role as President of the Movement of Non-Aligned Countries draws even more attention to Cuba's example. In October 1979, representing the Non-Aligned at the United Nations in New York, he bitterly attacked the unequal nature of world trade which makes poor nations still poorer. He condemned the "persistent chanelling of human and natural resources into the arms race, which is wasteful and dangerous to mankind". His two-hour speech finished with an impassioned appeal:

> Frequent mention is made of human rights, but mention should also be made of the rights of mankind.
> Why should some people go barefooted so that others may ride in expensive cars? Why should some live only 35 years so others may live to 70? Why should some be miserably poor so that others may be

exaggeratedly rich?

I speak on behalf of the world's children who do not even have a piece of bread; I speak on behalf of those who have been denied the right to life and human dignity.

Some countries are on the sea; others are not. Some have energy resources; others do not. Some possess abundant lands in which to produce foodstuffs; others do not. Some are so glutted with machinery and factories that you cannot even breathe the air of their poisoned atmospheres; others have only their emaciated arms with which to earn their bread.

In short, some countries possess abundant resources while others have nothing. What is their fate? To starve? To remain poor for ever? Why then civilization? Why then man's conscience? Why then the United Nations? You cannot speak of peace on behalf of tens of millions of human beings all over the world who are starving to death or dying of curable diseases. You cannot speak of peace on behalf of 900 million illiterate inhabitants. The exploitation of the poor countries by the rich countries must cease.

I address the rich nations, asking them to contribute. I address the poor countries, asking them to distribute.

Enough of words! We need deeds. Enough of abstraction! We need concrete action. Enough of speaking about a speculative new international economic order. Which nobody understands! We must speak about a real, objective order which everybody understands.

I have not come here as a prophet of the Revolution; nor have I come here to ask or wish that the world be violently convulsed. I have come to speak of peace and co-operation among the peoples, and I have come to warn that if we do not eliminate our present injustices and inequalities, peacefully, and wisely, the future will be apocalyptic.

Let us say farewell to arms, and let us dedicate ourselves in a civilised manner to the most pressing problems of our times. This is the responsibility and the most sacred duty of all the world's statesmen. Moreover, it is the basic premise for human survival.

Internal Developments

Fidel Castro's and Cuba's energies have not all been diverted to external efforts. Inside Cuba, there have been substantial developments throughout the 1960s and 1970s, resulting from investment and the dedication of energy in the 1960s.

In education, Cuba boasts 100 per cent attendance at elementary schools and about 80 per cent for secondary-age students. Figures that would delight any other Third World country are seen, in Cuba, as not yet good enough, and there is a campaign to ensure regular attendance at school for everyone. All Cuban schools combine study and work; at secondary level, students spend half their day in the classroom, the other half working in the school's fields. In inaugurating one of the "Schools in the Countryside" in May 1971, Fidel Castro explained its purpose:

> The idea [of the schools in the countryside] comprises two fundamental ideas both of them put forward by two great thinkers: Marx and Marti. Both conceived the school as linked to work, they conceived school as the centre where young men [and women] are prepared to face life and are formed in every respect; as the centre where man is formed integrally, where man is given an overall education.
>
> Ours is not a rich country .... Our education and medical services are way above what our material-economic base allows us. In other words, our expenses in education and public health are above our resources and our possibilities.
>
> If we were able to abide strictly by the available economic resources of our

40 A "School in the Countryside" given over to teach Angolan students in Cuba, one of many specially set aside for that purpose.

41 "School in the Countryside" students work in the fields.

country — a poor country, an underdeveloped country — we would not have as much as 25% of our population registered in school.

Our educational plan is way above our real economic possibility. Now then, could we possibly say: "Let only 50% of the young people study." No, we cannot do that, it would be an inhuman, an almost cruel thing to do.

Study and work are systematically combined.

Our country's progress will be determined by our success in education.

The production from these schools will practically cover the investment made in them, and their expenses.

Education is not only important for the young. Building on the 1961 Literacy Campaign, Castro started a new battle in Cuba, this time the "Battle for the Sixth Grade", to bring every adult up to sixth grade — elementary level) by 1980. Once this goal was reached, the battle for higher grades was begun because, as Fidel Castro has said:

42 Part of the "Battle for the Sixth Grade"; workers who are studying to catch up on the education they missed out on in the past.

We believe that anyone in tomorrow's world who hasn't passed the sixth grade will be an illiterate. For as everything is relative, he who signed by making his mark with his thumbprint 50 years ago was much more cultured than the man 20 or 30 years from now who has only a sixth grade education.

Sport in Cuba has been encouraged by the Revolution, with the aim of improving the welfare and recreation of the Cuban people. Since 1960 international successes in sport have brought considerable prestige to the country; in the unofficial rankings at the Montreal Olympics in 1976, Cubans came eighth in the world — in Rome in 1960, they had been forty-fifth.

Special sports schools have been set up for students with particular athletic gifts. Fidel Castro explained the thinking behind the establishment of one of these when he opened the "Martyrs of Barbados Sports

School" (named after those who died in the airliner sabotage in 1976) in 1977:

> We need champions because they become symbols of our young people and our children. Champions become the yardsticks of the social, educational and cultural development of our Revolution and our people.
>
> But, it's very important that we don't go wrong and neglect the practice of sports in our quest for champions. Everybody ought to practise sports — and not only children in elementary schools. Adults and old people too — even the old people — should practise sports. The old people need it more than the young. Young people need sports sometimes to burn off that extra energy they have: moreover sports are a means of developing discipline, education, health and good habits. Sports are an antidote to vice. Young people need sports. And old people, too, not to burn off excess energy but to conserve what energy they have left and to safeguard their health, which is so necessary to a full life.
>
> We can't allow any athlete in these schools to be a bad student.

Not all of Cuba's policies have yielded such immediately successful results. In the case of the liberation of women, the *machismo* which exists in Latin American societies and was strong in Cuba before the Revolution, is only slowly being eliminated. This has given little comfort to Fidel Castro who has championed the cause. He had some stirring words for the women of Cuba and their guests at the Second Congress of the Cuban Federation of Women in November 1974:

> On the question of prejudice, we told you once what happened in the Sierra Maestra when we went to organise the "Mariana Grajales" platoon, and the real resistance we encountered to the idea of arming the women's unit, which reminds us how much more backward we were a few years ago. Some men believed that women weren't capable of fighting. But the unit was organised and the women fought excellently, with all the bravery that the most valiant of our soldiers could have shown.
>
> Naturally, in the socialist countries woman has advanced a long distance along the road of her liberation. But if we ask ourselves about our own situation: we who are a socialist country with almost 16 years of revolution, can we really say that the Cuban woman has acquired full equality of rights in practice, and that she is absolutely integrated into Cuban society? . . .
>
> What must concern us as revolutionaries is that the work of the Revolution is not yet complete.

43 Fidel Castro takes every opportunity at schools and at factories to join in sports activities.

We believe that this struggle against discrimination of women, this struggle for women's equality and for women's integration, must be carried out by the whole society. And it is the task of our Party, in the first place; it is the task of our educational institutions, and it is the task of all our mass organisations.

Fidel Castro's Future Role in the Revolution

A question always asked is "What will happen to the Cuban Revolution when Fidel Castro goes?" Alas, none of us can see into the future. The institutionalization of the Revolution is designed to ensure that there are structures to maintain its momentum. And Fidel

44 The changing role of Cuban women has been supported in the press, through cartoons like this showing men doing what were considered to be traditionally women's jobs.

45 Members of the FMC, the Cuban Federation of Women, taking part in voluntary work.

Castro has said himself: "Men die, but the Party is immortal". He spoke of his future to the US journalist, Barbara Walters in 1977:

> As long as I am capable and can be useful at a post — this or any other — and the Revolution demands it of me, it is my duty to do the work. How long will it be? I don't know when I will die. I don't know whether it will be tomorrow or tonight, in an accident, or whether I will die a natural death — I can't know. Perhaps if I am capable up until I die, I will be on the job until then. If I'm going to have a long life, then most likely I won't be president until I die.

Two years later he modestly spoke of his own place in Cuban history to a group of young teachers:

> We don't see ourselves as monopolising the history of our country. Others made history before us; we have contributed modestly to that history; but perhaps the greatest, the most beautiful, the most moving history is yet to be written, and that is the history that you, the young, will make.

But on some matters he is absolutely unyielding, as he made clear at the inauguration of the National Assembly of People's Power in December 1976:

> I am a tireless critic of our own work. We could have done everything better from the Moncada attack up to today. The light that indicates what would have been the best choice in each case is experience, but unfortunately the youth who start along the hard and difficult road do not have it. Nevertheless, let us learn from this that we are not sages and that for each decision there might perhaps have been a better one.
>
> If I were to have the privilege of living my life again, I would do many things differently from the way I have done them up to now; but at the same time I can assure you that I would fight all my life with the same passion for the same objectives I have fought for up to now.

At the start of the 1980s, Fidel Castro is, in his early 50s, still a young man — much younger than most world statesmen. He has been in a position of power longer than anyone else on the world stage. With the enhanced position of Cuba in the world, the likelihood arises, through his Presidency and authority within the Non-Aligned Movement, that Fidel Castro's individual prestige will increase as the model of the Cuban Revolution is more widely applied. Few statesmen have lived to experience, as Castro has, the complete transformation of their country along lines determined by them. Cuba's success is Fidel Castro's success, too; it can be seen simply by comparing the economic, social and political development of Cuba with any other country in the world.

Cuba is not a perfect society, but it can claim areas of great advance, as Fidel Castro pointed out at the inauguration of the National Assembly of People's Power:

> Here [in Cuba] there are no differences, as in the bourgeois world, between military and civilians, whites and blacks, men and women, young and old, because all of us enjoy equal duties and rights. Nor are there, fortunately, differences between rich and poor, exploiters and exploited, powerful and humble, because the revolution eliminated the political power of the bourgeoisie and the big landowners to forge the workers' state. They are all our deputies; manual or intellectual workers, men and women, old and young, soldiers and civilians, who dedicate their lives to the service of the homeland and the revolution, or study and learn in order to be the heirs of our ideas, and our efforts and our struggles.

Date List

1946	January	Fidel Castro elected President of the Association of Law Students at Havana University.
1947	August-October	Fidel Castro joins Orthodox Party led by Eduardo Chibas. Fidel Castro involved in Key Confite expedition to liberate the Dominican Republic.
1948	April	Fidel Castro to the Conference of Latin American students in Bogota; involved in "Bogotazo" following assassination of Jorge Eliecer Gaitán.
1952	10 March	General Fulgencia Batista takes power in coup d'état.
	13 March	Fidel Castro lays charge against him in Supreme Court.
1953	26 July	Attack on Moncada Barracks in Santiago de Cuba led by Fidel Castro.
	16 October	Fidel Castro tried in camera; delivers "History Will Absolve Me" speech; sentenced to 15 years in prison; reunited with other "Moncadistas" in El Presidio prison on Isle of Pines.
1954		Fidel Castro organizes M26J from prison cell.
1955	May	"Moncadistas" freed in amnesty.
	7 July	Fidel Castro leaves for exile in Mexico, where he meets Ernesto Che Guevara.
1956	September	Fidel Castro breaks links with Orthodox Party; signs agreement with José Antonio Echeverria, leader of Revolutionary Directorate.
	25 November	*Granma* leaves Tuxpan, Mexico, with 82 armed rebels aboard.
	30 November	Uprising in Santiago de Cuba led by Frank Pais and Pepito Tey, who is killed in the action.
	2 December	*Granma* lands in Cuba.
	5 December	Batista's army surprises Fidel Castro and *Granma* expeditionaries.
	18-25 December	Fidel Castro and remainder of his group reunited to form the first guerilla group.
1957	17 January	Successful attack on the La Plata Barracks.
	17 February	Fidel Castro interviewed by Herbert Mathews of *New York Times* (published 28 Feb.)

	13 March	Revolutionary Directorate attack Presidential Palace, José Antonio Echeverria killed; wave of repression by Batista; action condemned by Fidel Castro.
	March	Frank Pais sends Fidel Castro 50 recruits from Santiago.
	28 May	Attack on El Uvero Barracks.
	30 July	Frank Pais killed in Santiago.
	August	West of Cuba paralysed by General Strike; 2nd Rebel Column set up by Fidel Castro, led by Ernesto Che Guevara.
	3 September	Sailors revolt in Cienfuegos; bombed by Batista's troops.
1958	January-March	Series of attacks and sabotage in Havana; no electricity or water for 3 days; airport burnt down.
	10 March	Raul Castro opens 2nd Front called "Frank Pais Front" in Northern Oriente.
	12 March	Fidel Castro calls for General Strike, to withhold taxes and keep off highways after 1 April.
	9 April	General Strike collapses.
	5 May	Fidel Castro recognized as sole leader of M26J.
	May-July	Batista launches massive army attack on rebels.
	July-August	Rebel counter-offensive led by Fidel Castro.
	29 August	Column led by Che Guevara and Camilo Cienfuegos invades plains of Camagüey and Las Villas.
	September	Fidel Castro's troops take Oriente.
	24 December	Che Guevara's column moves towards Santa Clara, capital of Las Villas.
	31 December	Santa Clara garrison surrenders.
1959	"Year of Liberation"	
	1 January	Batista flees Cuba.
	2 January	Fidel Castro takes Santiago de Cuba. Havana under control by Rebel Army, led by Che Guevara and Camilo Cienfuegos.
	3 January	Castro appointed Commander-in-Chief of Army.
	8 January	Fidel Castro arrives in Havana. Speaks from Camp Columbia.
	13 February	Becomes Prime Minister following resignation of Miro Cardona.
	15 April	Fidel Castro in Washington, USA, on "unofficial" visit; meets Vice-President Nixon.
	17 May	Fidel Castro signs Agrarian Reform Law.
	June	First diplomatic note from USA expressing "concern" over Agrarian Reform.
	18 June	Castro resigns as Prime Minister over difficulties with President Urrutia. Osvaldo Dorticos becomes President.
	24 June	Castro again Prime Minister.
	29 October	Camilo Cienfuegos lost in plane.
1960	"Year of Agrarian Reform"	
	4 February	Anastas Mikoyan arrives to open Soviet exhibition in Havana.
	13 February	First Cuban/USSR agreement.
	4 March	*La Coubre* explosion in Havana; 75 dead.
	23 April	Fidel Castro accuses USA of planning aggression against Cuba.
	1 May	Fidel Castro names brother Raul as successor.

	8 May	Cuba/USSR diplomatic relations established.
	22 June	USA cuts sugar quota.
	23 July	China/Cuba economic agreement.
	28 August	Cuba leaves OAS.
	2 September	Fidel Castro announces 1st Declaration of Havana.
	18 September	Fidel Castro arrives in New York for United Nations General Assembly.
	27 September	Cuba recognizes People's Republic of China.
	15 October	Cuban government nationalizes major enterprises and banks.
	19 October	US embargo on goods to Cuba.
	24 October	Cuba nationalizes remaining 166 US companies in Cuba.
	1 November	Raul Roa, Cuban Foreign Minister, accuses USA of planning Cuban invasion.
1961	"Year of Education"	
	3 January	USA breaks diplomatic links with Cuba.
	February	Che Guevara Minister of Industry.
		Cuban media warn of US invasion.
	10 April	Literacy Campaign officially begun.
	16 April	Castro announces Cuban Revolution is "socialist".
	17 April	Bay of Pigs Invasion begins.
	20 April	Bay of Pigs Invasion defeated. Some 1,200 prisoners taken.
	25 April	Total embargo by USA on all trade to Cuba.
	2 December	Fidel Castro declares "I am a Marxist, and shall remain one until the end of my life."
1962	"Year of Planning"	
	10 January	Cuba/USSR trade agreement; $700 million trade in 1962.
	31 January	OAS excludes Cuba.
	4 February	Fidel Castro makes 2nd Declaration of Havana.
	12 March	Rationing of essential items introduced.
	21-28 October	US President Kennedy reveals presence of Soviet missiles in Cuba.
	30 October	U Thant, Secretary-General of United Nations, in Havana.
	2 November	Dismantled missiles return to USSR. Mikoyan in Cuba.
	20 November	Quarantine of Cuba called off by USA.
	21 December	USA agrees to supply Cuba with equipment and medicines in exchange for Bay of Pigs prisoners.
1963	"Year of Organization"	
	21 March	Fidel Castro rebukes Kruschev over action during missile crisis.
	27 April	Fidel Castro fêted on visit to USSR.
	3, 4 June	Fidel Castro announces new economic agreement with USSR.
	5-7 October	Hurricane Flora devastates East of Cuba.
1964	"Year of the Economy"	
	7 January	British Leyland sells 450 buses to Cuba.
	13-14 January	Fidel Castro to USSR for second time; declares Cuba will produce 10 million tons of sugar in 1970.
	18 February	USA cuts military aid to Britain and France for trading with Cuba.

	19 April	Castro objects to US U2 flights over Cuba.
	29 June	Fidel Castro's sister defects to USA.
	9 December	Che Guevara addresses General Assembly of United Nations.
1965	**"Year of Agriculture"**	
	1 January	Che Guevara in Congo, Brazzaville.
	14 February	Fidel Castro takes command of Agrarian Reform Institute and Ministry of Agriculture.
	7 June	Fidel Castro applauds sugar "Zafra".
	25 September	Castro announces Cubans free to leave for USA.
	20 April	Che Guevara disappears; Fidel Castro announces: "He will be found where he is most useful to the Revolution."
	3 October	Fidel Castro introduces Central Committee of PCC to Cuba and reads Che's farewell letter.
1966	**"Year of Solidarity"**	
	3-15 January	Tricontinental Conference in Havana; OSPAAL founded (Organization for Solidarity with the People of Africa, Asia and Latin America).
	6 February	Castro accuses China of reneging on rice deal: "China has abused the faith of the Cuban people."
	28 September	Fidel Castro denounces "Those who have nothing but pesos in their heads"; speaks in favour of moral incentives.
1967	**"Year of Heroic Viet Nam"**	
	28 January	Fidel Castro renounces copyright convention.
	April	Che's message to Tricontinental: "Create one, two, three, many Viet Nams."
	31 July	Organization of Latin American solidarity open in Cuba; calls for "violent revolution" in hemisphere.
	8 October	Che Guevara killed in Bolivia.
	15-18 October	National mourning for Che.
1968	**"Year of the Heroic Guerilla"**	
	2 January	Fidel Castro announces austerity measures, tighter petrol rationing.
	4-11 January	Cultural Congress in Havana; Fidel Castro attacks "pseudo-revolutionaries".
	3 February	Annibal Escalante of the Microfaction sentenced to 15 years' imprisonment.
	13 March	Fidel Castro launches "Revolutionary Offensive".
	2 August	Fidel Castro approves Soviet intervention in Czechoslovakia.
1969	**"Year of Decisive Force"**	
	2 January	Fidel Castro announces sugar rationing.
	9 July	Fidel Castro approves the Revolutionary step taken by the Military Junta in Peru.
	December	US volunteers, the "Venceremos Brigade", arrive in Cuba, to help with 10 million tons "Zafra". Vietnamese brigade for same purpose.
1970	**"Year of the 10 Million Tons"**	
	June	Cuban volunteers send blood to Peruvian earthquake.

	15 June	Zafra ends. 8½ million tons of 10 million target achieved.
	26 July	Fidel Castro makes "Autocritica" and warns of hardships.
	12 November	Salvador Allende's government in Chile recognizes Cuba.

1971 "Year of Productivity"

	November	Fidel Castro in Chile for 4-week visit.

1972 "Year of Socialist Emulation"

	May-June	Fidel Castro visits 10 African and European countries.
	8 July	Cuba and Peru re-establish diplomatic relations.

1973 "Year of the 20th Anniversary" (of the Moncada attack)

	5 February	Cuba, USA and Canada sign 5-year anti-hijacking agreement.
	28 May	Argentina recognizes Cuba.
	12 September	Chilean Junta break relations with Cuba.

1974 "Year of the 15th Anniversary" (of the Success of the Revolution)

	28 January	Leonid Brezhnev, General Secretary of the Communist Party of the USSR, visits Cuba.
	30 June	Election for Municipal Assemblies in Matanzas.
	25 November	Fidel Castro presides over 2nd Congress of the Federation of Cuban Women.

1975 "Year of the First Congress"

	26 February	Drafting Committee returns draft Constitution to Fidel Castro.
	7-22 December	First Congress of Cuban Communist Party; Fidel Castro as First Secretary of the Party; gives main report lasting 10 hours in total; Fidel Castro and Raul Castro ratified as First and Second Secretaries of the Central Committee.

1976 Year of the 20th Anniversary of the "Granma"

	5 January	Draft Constitution published.
	15 February	97% vote yes to new Socialist Constitution.
	26 February-16 March	Fidel Castro speaks at 25th Congress of CPSU in Moscow.
	13 August	Fidel Castro's 50th birthday; awarded Order of the October Revolution by President of Supreme Soviet of USSR.
	6 October	Cubana de Aviaciones DC8 sabotaged off Barbados; 73 people on board killed.
	2 November	Fidel and Raul Castro elected deputies to the National Assembly of People's Power.

1977 "Year of Institutionalization"

	28 February-8 April	Fidel Castro travels to Africa, Asia and Europe.
	16-20 October	Fidel Castro makes friendly visit to Jamaica.

1978 "Year of the 11th (Youth) Festival"

	28 July-5 August	11th Youth Festival in Havana, presided over by Fidel Castro.
	11-20 September	Fidel Castro visits Ethiopia, Libya and Algeria.

1979 "20th Year of Victory"

	14 April	Cuba and Grenada establish diplomatic relations.
	16-18 May	Fidel Castro in Mexico.
	3-9 September	6th Summit Conference of the Movement of Non-Aligned Countries opens in Havana; Fidel Castro elected Chairman and makes opening speech.
	10 September	Hurricane Frederick hits Cuba.

September-October	"Caribbean Crisis" over Soviet troops in Cuba; "There has been no change in the nature or in the function of the Soviet personnel in Cuba in the past 17 years" (Fidel Castro).
2 October	Fidel Castro to New York to address the 34th session of the United Nations General Assembly as Chairman of the Non-Aligned Countries Movement.

1980 **"Year of the 2nd Congress"**

11 January	Celia Sanchez dies after 25 years as close friend and comrade of Fidel Castro.

Biographical Notes on Fidel Castro's Contemporaries

Fulgencia Batista (1901-1973)
Batista was twice President of Cuba, from 1940-44, and from 1952, when he took power by force, to 1959, when he fled the country, politically and militarily defeated by Fidel Castro and the Rebel Army who were advancing on Havana. Batista was a sergeant in the Cuban Army before becoming President in 1940, having led the so-called "Sergeants' Revolt" in 1933, which toppled President Cespedes. The corruption and brutality of his period of office from 1952 lost him any support he may have had with the people. He fled to the Dominican Republic in 1959 and from there to Spain, where he died peacefully in 1973.

Lindon Forbes Samson Burnham (1923 -)
London-trained lawyer. Premier of British-Guyana from 1964-66, Prime Minister from 1966, made the first executive President of Guyana in 1980. Leader of the People's National Congress Party (PNC).

Raul Castro
Younger brother of Fidel Castro, participated in the Moncada attack in 1953, was imprisoned on the Isle of Pines, exiled in Mexico and returned to Cuba on board the *Granma* in 1956. Raul Castro is 2nd Secretary of the PCC, 1st Vice-President of the Council of State, and General of the Army.

Eduardo Chibas (1907-1951)
Leader of the Cuban Orthodox Party. Committed suicide during a radio programme in 1951, as a result of an argument with the Minister of Education whom he had accused of corruption.

Camilo Cienfuegos (19   -1959)
A major in the Rebel Army who, with Che Guevara, led the offensive against Las Villas in 1958. The following year he was lost over the sea, en route to Havana by plane. Fidel Castro led the unsuccessful search for Camilo and the other passengers. "Black propaganda" from outside Cuba accused Fidel Castro of Camilo's death (repeated in a British newspaper in 1981), though he was one of Fidel Castro's most loyal officers. His disappearance is commemorated each October in Cuba, when schoolchildren throw flowers into the sea.

José Antonio Echeverria (19   -1957)
Student leader of Havana University, and member of the Revolutionary Directorate which attacked the Presidential Palace in 1957. In the incident he was killed in a gunfight with police outside Radio Reloj, after prematurely broadcasting the news that Batista was dead.

Dwight D. Eisenhower (1890-1967)
Commander of Allied Forces in Europe

during the Second World War, became USA's 34th President in 1952. He was still President of the USA, with Richard M. Nixon as Vice-President, at the start of the Cuban Revolution. Refused to meet Fidel Castro during his visits to the USA in 1959, preferring to play golf, but agreed to Nixon's proposal that the CIA be charged to draw up invasion plans of Cuba to topple the new regime led by Fidel Castro.

Calixto Garcia (-1899)
General in the 10 Years War (1868-1878) against Spain and leader of the Cuban exile movement, the Cuban Revolutionary Committee, returning to Cuba in 1895 as one of the leaders of the successful campaign against Spain. Died during a visit to Washington, 1899.

Grau San Martin (1887-1969)
President of Cuba from September 1933-January 1944, and from 1944 to 1948.

Ernesto Che Guevara (1928-1967)
One of the great revolutionary heroes. Che was an Argentinian doctor who had travelled widely throughout Latin America in 1953 and '54, and had come to the conclusion that a radical change was necessary. Met Fidel Castro in Mexico in 1955 and joined his group travelling to Cuba on board the *Granma*. Che was "toothpuller" and doctor in the Rebel Army, as well as showing considerable military skill. He was made a Major, the highest rank, in the Rebel Army and led the 1958 attack on the Escambray region in Central Cuba and on Las Villas. He held a number of posts in the Revolutionary government: Minister of Industries, President of the National Bank, but was unsuited to bureaucratic work and left Cuba in 1965 to support the revolutionary struggle elsewhere in Latin America. He was killed in Bolivia, 7 October 1967.

John F. Kennedy (1917-1963)
Youngest President of the USA from 1961 until his assassination in 1963. Approved the attack on the Bay of Pigs in 1961; tough negotiator in 1962 with Chairman Kruschev during the Missile Crisis. President Kennedy is known to have attempted to bring about a rapprochement with Cuba: on the day of his assassination a French journalist met with Fidel Castro with messages from President Kennedy. Fidel Castro has emphatically denied any Cuban involvement in the assassination, although evidence does point in the direction of disaffected Cuban emigré groups in the USA dissatisfied with Kennedy's lack of action over Cuba.

Robert Kennedy (1925-1968)
Younger brother of J.F. Kennedy and Attorney General at the time of the Missile Crisis about which he has written in *13 Days, The Cuban Missile Crisis*. Assassinated 5 June 1968.

Nikita Kruschev (1894-1971)
Stalin's Viceroy over the Ukraine from 1938 until his recall to Moscow in 1949. Saw chance of power with Stalin's death in 1953. Denounced Stalin at the 20th Party Congress in 1956. Became Chairman of the Soviet Union in 1958. Kruschev had many meetings with the Cuban leadership, including Fidel Castro, during the early 1960s. He did not confer with Fidel Castro in 1962 during the decisions to dismantle Soviet missile bases in Cuba.

Antonio Maceo (1845-1896)
Black leader of Cuba's independence struggle, named "The Bronze Titan". Camilo Cienfuegos' invasion of the Western Provinces in 1958 was a duplicate of Maceo's in 1895. Maceo fought in the 10 Years War and the Second War of Independence from 1895. He is famous for his "Protest of Baragua" in 1878, when he refused to surrender at the end of the 10 Years War. Maceo's mother, Mariana Grajales, is famous in Cuba for her sacrifices during the independence struggle.

Michael Manley (1924 -)

Prime Minister of Jamaica from 19 to 1980, Manley developed a close relationship with Fidel Castro through the Non-Aligned Countries Movement. He visited Cuba in 1975. Economic agreements were signed between the two governments, resulting in collaboration in health, education, fishing, sport, tourism, as well as in a number of hydraulic and construction projects. The programme was scaled down after October 1980, when Manley lost the election to Edward Seaga, who is much closer to the USA.

José Martí (1853-1895)

Known as "The Apostle" of Cuba's independence struggle, Martí was a poet, playwright, novelist and journalist as well as a skilful orator, organizer, and revolutionary. In 1869 he was arrested for treason and the next year imprisoned, forced to do hard labour on the Isle of Pines, which considerably affected his health. In 1871 he was deported to Spain and, although able to return to Cuba in 1879, he soon returned to Spain where he studied law in Madrid and Zaragoza. Martí did not set foot on Cuban soil again until 1895. He spent the 1880s mostly in New York and travelling throughout Latin America, "Our America" as he described it. By 1887 he was head of the Provisional Executive Committee, a group of exile forces against Spain. With the formation of the Cuban Revolutionary Party in 1892, Martí was made "Delegate", the equivalent of President. Tireless in his organizing, he brought together all the disparate forces opposed to Spain. His first plans to invade Cuba in January 1895 were revealed to the authorities in Florida and the boats and arms were confiscated. But by April he had organized another invasion and landed in Cuba. Martí was killed in his first battle, on 19 May 1895. Martí was a very advanced thinker for his day and had a considerable influence on later generations of Cubans. Fidel Castro described him as "the intellectual author of the Moncada attack".

Anastas J. Mikoyan (1895-1978)

People's Commissar on Foreign Trade in the USSR, Mikoyan led many delegations to Western countries, as he did to Cuba in 1961, to negotiate trade agreements. Retired after Kruschev's fall from power in 1964.

Richard M. Nixon (1913-)

US Vice-President to Dwight Eisenhower in 1959 at the time of the triumph of the Cuban Revolution, and later President of the USA himself (1968-74). Met Fidel Castro in April 1959 and was convinced that he was a "Communist" or "under Communist domination". Nixon was hostile towards Cuba and the Cuban Revolution from then on, probably because of his friendship with Batista and other Cubans who subsequently left Cuba. Nixon was especially hated in Cuba because of his policies in Southeast Asia and his name was always printed with a swastika instead of an "x" in the press. His disgrace and resignation in the 1974 Watergate Affair led to the publication of details of American assassination attempts on the life of Fidel Castro and other Cuban leaders.

Frank Pais (1932-1957)

A young Baptist schoolmaster in Santiago who led the M26J in Oriente. He led the "action groups" in Cuba while Fidel Castro was in Mexico. It was Frank Pais who organized the uprising in Santiago on 30 November and 1 December 1956 to coincide with the arrival of the *Granma* which had, unfortunately, been held up by bad weather. Frank Pais was a tireless organizer on behalf of M26J and was shot dead in the streets of Santiago by the Cuban Chief of Police.

Carlos Prio Soccaras (1903-1980)

President of Cuba from 1948-52. Member of the Autentico Party. Carlos Prio's presidency is remembered for the corruption and gangsterism which pervaded it and which he condoned. To justify his own illegal seizure of power in 1952, Batista claimed that

Prio was also planning a coup, in order to remain in power.

Abel Santamaria (-1953)
2nd in Command of the attack on the Moncada Barracks in 1953. Abel, a "fanatic of Martí", was a close friend of Fidel Castro and brother to Haydee Santamaria who also took part in the Moncada attack. Captured by the police, he was tortured to death.

Adlai Stevenson (1900-1965)
US Ambassador to the United Nations for both President Kennedy and his successor, President Johnson. He was in office at the time of the Bay of Pigs crisis in 1961, when he was misled by his President. During the Missile Crisis of the following year it was said that he was able to get his own back.

Rafael Leonidas Trujillo (1891-1961)
Dictator of the Dominican Republic, installed by US Marines after their invasion of Santo Domingo in 1924. In 1927 he was Commander of the National Police, then President from 1930 until 1952, except for the period 1938-42 when he still controlled events. His regime is marked by its corruption and brutality. Assassinated in mysterious circumstances in 1961.

Ramiro Valdes
"Moncadista", in exile with Fidel Castro, returned as one of the 82 on the *Granma*. After the Revolution he was Commander of troops in Las Villas, and later Minister of the Interior.

Glossary

Alliance for Progress
Proposed by President John F. Kennedy during his election campaign in 1959 and discussed and agreed upon by the Organization of American States (OAS) meeting in Punta del Este, Uruguay in August 1961. In its first ten years $10 billion were invested in Latin American countries, provided by the USA, charities and international organizations. Primarily designed to bring about social development in Latin America, the Alliance was also a way of trying to ensure that there were no more Cubas on the continent. The main beneficiaries in the 1960s were right-wing dictatorships, resulting in a reduction in human rights and the aggravation of social inequalities.

Battle for the Sixth Grade
A development of Cuba's 1961 Literacy Campaign. The Battle for the Sixth Grade was a plan to bring every adult up to a sixth grade (elementary) level of education by 1980. Supported by the CTC (Cuban Federation of Workers), it was claimed a complete success in mid-1979. The Battle for the Eighth Grade was immediately begun.

Blockade
More accurately an "embargo" imposed by the USA in 1960 on all trade to and from Cuba. The ban applies to all US companies as well as to OAS member countries and many allies of the USA in Europe. It was hugely successful in the first years of the Revolution, as almost all machinery, cars, and other equipment for Cuba had been "made in USA". Its effect was less by the end of the 1960s and 1970s when most Cuban industry and equipment had been replaced. The "blockade" was still in existence at the start of the 1980s and regarded by the Cuban government as an example of "genocide", of the US trying to starve out Cuban people.

Brigadistas
Members of a "Brigada", a Brigade. The most famous Brigade was the Conrado Benitez Brigade, named after a young literacy teacher killed by counter-revolutionaries during the 1961 Literacy Campaign. Many young people still go to Cuba to participate in construction and agricultural Brigades: the Venceremos Brigade from the USA, the Antonio Maceo made up of Cubans in the USA, the José Marti Brigade from Western Europe, and the Nordic Brigade from Scandinavia. Cuban "Brigadistas" work as teachers in schools, and many have gone to African countries and to Nicaragua to assist with literacy campaigns there.

CDRs — Committees for the Defence of the Revolution
Founded in September 1960 during a speech by Fidel Castro, as bombs were heard to go

off in Havana. Originally formed as grass-roots security organizations to combat counter-revolutionary sabotage, they are now just as important as community-based social organizations responsible for the maintenance of each area, collecting recyclable materials, ensuring children's attendance at school, as well as arranging discussion groups after important political speeches.

CIA — Central Intelligence Agency
The security agency of the US government, responsible for gathering intelligence information and performing aggressive acts against other nations and individuals. Formed out of the Office of Strategic Services (OSS) in 1942, the CIA came into existence in 1947 with the National Security Act. The CIA were responsible for the débâcle at the Bay of Pigs in 1961 and for the assassination attempts on Fidel Castro and other government leaders.

Demajagua
The bell of the Demajagua sugar plantation, in Oriente Province, was rung in 1868 to signal the start of the offensive against the Spanish and the start of the 10 Years War.

DR — Directorio Revolucionario (Revolutionary Directorate)
An urban-based revolutionary group operating mainly in Havana from 1957. It was integrated into the ORI in 1961. Anti-Communist, the DR did not follow the line of the M26J, preferring a town-based organization. Responsible for the attack on the Presidential Palace in 1957.

FMC — Cuban Federation of Women
The FMC united all existing women's organizations into one in 1960. Its objective is to raise the level of political, ideological, cultural and scientific achievement for all women, so as to facilitate their participation in all areas of the Cuban Revolution. 85 per cent of women in Cuba, over the age of 16 years, belong to the FMC, and there is no area of Cuba however remote, without FMC members.

Guantánamo
On 1 January 1899 Spain's sovereignty over Cuba ended and that of the USA began. In 1903 the Platt Amendment was presented to the US Senate and in March became law. This gave the USA the right to "intervene for the preservation of life, property, and individual liberty" as well as to take "lands necessary for naval stations". The USA took possession of the land and sea areas around Guantánamo, in Oriente, at a price of $2,000 in US gold. The land no longer has any military or strategic value to the US, other than serving as a constant source of annoyance, and possible danger, to the Cuban people. Since the start of the Revolution the Cuban government has not accepted payment for nor provided water, electricity, or other services to the base. It is periodically "re-invaded" by the USA, as in 1979 and 1981, in times of crisis.

M26J — the July 26th Movement
M26J took its name from the date of the attack on the Moncada Barracks in 1953 and was formed during Fidel Castro's imprisonment and on his release from prison in 1955.

Machismo
The Spanish, and Latin American, tradition that gives greater importance to the role of men in society than to the role of women. The man, traditionally, works; the woman, unless very poor, stays at home and looks after the house and children. "Everything goes" for the man whereas the woman is supposed to lead a submissive life. These attitudes are being combated in Cuba.

Moncada Manifesto
The revolutionary programme written by Fidel Castro which was to have been broadcast to the nation after the attack on Moncada, 26 July 1953, had it been successful.

Moncadistas
The name given to the participants in the

attack on the Moncada Barracks, 26 July 1953. Many surviving Moncadistas occupy leading government posts.

Movement of Non-Aligned Countries

Formed in April 1961 by Tito of Yugoslavia and Nasser of Egypt. The countries involved were predominantly Afro-Asian, concerned with de-colonization and keeping the "Great Powers" out of Africa and Asia. The Movement has greatly expanded since its formation. The 1979 Havana Summit was preceded by Belgrade, 1961; Cairo, 1964; Lusaka, 1970; Algiers, 1973; Colombo, 1976. Fidel Castro was made Chairman for 5 years in 1979.

OAS — the Organization of American States

The first Pan-American Conference was held in 1889. This organization became the Pan-American Union, then the OAS in 1948. The USA attended the first meeting of the organization as observer, but soon assumed its hegemony and the OAS now closely follows US policy in Latin America. Cuba was expelled from the OAS in 1961, and economic sanctions were applied, at the request of the USA. In the 1970s OAS member nations were given the individual right to restore relations with Cuba.

Orthodox Party

Also known as the Cuban People's Party. Formed as a breakaway from the Autentico Party in May 1947, with Eduardo Chibas as leader.

PCC — Partido Communista Cubano (Cuban Communist Party)

Existed before the Revolution as the Partido Socialista Popular (PSP), the Popular Socialist Party. Few of its members were involved in the insurrection led by Fidel Castro, whom they considered an "adventurist". In 1961 the ORI (Integrated Revolutionary Organization) was formed, bringing all the different political parties under one umbrella. Then, in 1963, the PURS, the United Party of the Socialist Revolution, was formed, which established a party political structure. The PCC was formed in 1965.

Playa Giron (The Bay of Pigs)

Site of the invasion by Cuban exiles and mercenaries, trained and funded by the CIA, in April 1961. Their defeat is claimed by Cuba to be "the first defeat of imperialism in Latin America". Fidel Castro personally directed military operations against the invaders who were repulsed in 72 hours. The prisoners taken included criminals from Batista's time, who were subsequently put on trial. The great majority of the prisoners were exchanged for medicines and baby foods, the US government having refused their exchange for tractors. Fidel Castro was later to claim that the US "cheated" on the deal.

Poder Popular (People's Power)

System of participatory democracy applied to the whole of Cuba in 1976, having been tried in Matanzas in 1974. Direct elections take place for "Delegates" at Municipal level, with indirect elections to Provincial and National Assemblies. Delegates are required to "render accounts" periodically with their electors and if found wanting are dismissed from their posts. The introduction of Poder Popular was part of the "Institutionalization of the Revolution".

Radio Rebelde (Rebel Radio)

The Rebel Army's radio station operating from the Sierra Maestra from 1957. Radio Rebelde played an important part in the revolutionary struggle, as it gave Fidel Castro and the M26J a means of communicating with the Cuban people when Batista operated press censorship.

Radio Reloj (Clock Radio)

Still in existence in Cuba, Radio Reloj intersperses news items with minute-by-minute time checks. This was the station taken by José Antonio Echeverria during the 1957 attack on the Presidential Palace, in order to broadcast, prematurely, news of the death of Batista.

Schools in the Countryside

Escuelas en el Campo (Schools in the Countryside) are the model for secondary education in Cuba. They result from experiments in the 1960s taking Schools *to* the Countryside. These were so successful that Schools *in* the Countryside were adopted in 1970. All schools are similarly constructed, co-educational, boarding schools for about 500 students, who study and also work on the 1,300 hectares of land around the school. On the Isle of Youth the work done by students is largely in the citrus plantations, but in other schools a wide range of agricultural work is done. Other co-educational boarding schools are Cuba's Vocational Schools, attended only by the "best of the best" students, and the EIDEs, Sports Schools, which combine study and sport.

Sierra Maestra

The highest mountain range in Cuba, in the east of the country, which provided cover and support for the M26J from 1957-59. The peasant farmers, who frequently lived a semi-criminal life themselves, gave Fidel Castro and the Rebel Army much-needed support. In return, the Rebel Army paid them for all foodstuffs provided, as well as giving medical treatment and setting up the first schools in the area. The first Agrarian Reform, which gave land to the small farmers, was signed by Fidel Castro in the Sierra Maestra.

U2

High-altitude "spy plane" used by the CIA to gather information over Cuba as well as the Soviet Union. During the 1962 Missile Crisis a U2 was shot down over Cuba, with the loss of its pilot. Western press sources claimed in 1981 that Fidel Castro had personally fired the missile that brought it down. Another U2 had been similarly shot down by a missile over the USSR on 1 May 1960.

War of Independence

Cuba's Revolution is seen as the culmination of a Hundred Years of Struggle for independence, which began in 1868 with the 10 Years War, the Little War of 1879 and the successful war against Spain from 1895. This brought the USA into the country through a mysterious explosion on board the USS *Maine* in Havana harbour.

Zafra

Cuban term for the sugar harvest, which lasts from December through to April or May.

Some Suggestions for Further Reading

On Fidel Castro

Castro: A political biography by Herbert Mathews (Allen Lane/Penguin, 1969)
Castro's Cuba, Cuba's Fidel by Lee Lockwood (Vintage, 1969)
Fidel Castro by Enrique Meneses (Faber & Faber, 1968)
Fidel Castro Speaks Edited by Martin Kenner & James Petras (Penguin, 1970)
Revolutionary Struggle: The Collected Works of Fidel Castro Vol. 1. Edited by Rolando Bonachea & Nelson P. Valdes (MIT, 1972)
With Fidel by Frank Mankiewicz and Kirby Jones (Ballantine Books, 1975)

General Books on Cuba

Anatomy of a Revolution by Huberman and Sweezy (Monthly Review, 1960)
Cuba for Beginners by Rius (Writers & Readers, 1977)
Cuba: The Second Decade edited by John Griffiths & Peter Griffiths (Writers & Readers, 1979)
Socialism in Cuba by Huberman & Sweezy (Monthly Review, 1968)

Granma, a weekly review of Cuba's national daily newspaper, is available from:
Collet's Holdings Ltd
Subscription Import Dept,
Denington Estate,
Wellingborough,
Northants
NN8 2PT.

Visual Aids

Slides on Cuba dealing with "The Economy", "Culture", "Education System", "Political System", and "A History of Cuba", as well as a set on "Fidel Castro", are available from:
  The Slide Centre Ltd
  143 Chatham Road,
  London
  SW11 6SR.

The films *Fidel* (by Saul Landau), *The Battle for the Ten Million* (by Chris Marker) and many Cuban Documentary films are available from:
  The Other Cinema,
  79 Wardour Street,
  London
  W1 3TH

Numerous Cuban documentary and feature films are distributed by:
  Contemporary Films Ltd,
  55, Greek Street,
  London
  W1.

The film *Cuba Si* (by Chris Marker) and Cuban feature films are distributed by:
  Connoisseur Films Ltd,
  167, Oxford Street,
  London
  W1.

Index

Numbers in **bold type** refer to pages on which illustrations appear

Africa, Cuban relations, 59, 61, 63
agrarian reform, 28
agriculture, 41f
Allende, Salvador, 57
Alliance for Progress, 43, 81
assassination attempts on Fidel Castro, 59f

Barbados, 59
Batista, Fulgencia, 9, 77; **9**
   defeat and flight from Cuba, 24f
   escape from Presidential Palace, 22
   Fidel Castro's attack on, 17
   freeing of "Moncadistas", 16
   Granma landing, 19
   Herbert Mathews' article, 22
Battle for the Sixth Grade, 67, 81
Bay of Pigs, *see* Playa Giron
Bayamo, 11f
Bayo, Alberto, 18
Blockade, of Cuba, 37, 57, 58, 81
Bogota, 8
"Bogotazo", 8f
Bohemia, 16
Bolivia, 47
Burnham, Forbes, 62, 77

Caribbean Conference of Churches, 61-62
Castro, Fidel, **2, 13, 21**
   attack on the Presidential Palace, 23
   Bay of Pigs, 34f
   "Bogotazo", 8
   Camp Columbia speech, 26
   and Che Guevara, 18, 47f
   on Communism and the Cuban Communist Party, 28, 55
   on Cuban/African relations, 63
   declaration of Cuba's socialist path, 31, 36
   Declaration of Havana, 45f
   denunciation of Batista, 9
   on education, 65
   exile in Mexico, 17ff
   "History Will Absolve Me", 13
   importance of his speeches, 26
   and industrialization, 40
   interview with Herbert Mathews, 22
   invasion of the Dominican Republic, 8
   and Latin America, 57
   and Literacy Campaign, 33
   Moncada attack, 10ff
   and New Man, 48
   President of Non-Aligned Movement, 64
   in prison, 15ff
   "Report on the Offensive", 23
   speech to the people of Santiago de Cuba, 25
   and sport, 68
   and 10 Million Tons, 49ff; **50**
   and UN General Assembly, 27f, **61**
   and USA, 27f, 30, 43ff, 59
   and Women's Rights, 68
Castro, Raul, 13, 63, 77; **53**
Central Intelligence Agency (CIA), 30, 59, 60, 82; **60**
Chibas, Eduardo, 8f, 77
Chile, Fidel Castro's visit, 7; **58**
Cienfuegos, Camilo, 26, 77; **26**
Committees for the Defence of the Revolution (CDRs), 54, 81; **54**
Communist Party of Cuba, 54f, 83
   Congress of, 55
Constitution, 55f
coup d'état, 10 March 1952, 9
coup d'état, attempt 1 January 1959, 25

Declaration of Havana, 45
Demajagua, Bell of, 8, 82
development, 39, 65
Directorio Revolucionario (DR), *see* Revolutionary Directorate
Dominican Republic, 8

Echeverria, José Antonio, 23, 77
education, 65
Eisenhower, Dwight D., 29, 30, 77
El Caney, 12
El Presidio prison, 15
El Salvador, 62f
El Uvero, battle of, 23
Escambray Mountains, 31

"Family Code", 55
FMC (Cuban Federation of Women), 54, 82; **69**
Ford, Gerald, 59

Gaitán, Jorge Eliecer, 9
Garcia, Calixto, 25, 78
Granma (Cuba's daily newspaper), 11
Granma (yacht), purchase, 18
   journey to Cuba, 19
Grau, San Martin, 8, 78
Grenada 62
Guantánamo, 38, 82
Guatemala, 30, 31
Guevara, Ernesto "Che", 18, 26, 28, 47; **20, 43, 47**
   in Bolivia, 46f
   on Fidel Castro's speeches, 27
   on industrialization, 39f
Guyana, 62

Havana,
   University, 7
   Presidential Palace attack, 22
Hernandez, Melba, 16
"History Will Absolve Me", 13ff

incentives, moral and material, 52
industrialization plans, 39, 40
Institutionalization, 55, 59 (*see also* People's Power)

Jamaica, relations with Cuba, 61f

Kennedy, John F., 30, 78
   statement on Cuba, 30
   after the Bay of Pigs invasion, 33
   and Cuban exiles, 35
   at Missile Crisis, 35f
Kennedy, Robert, on Missile Crisis, 35, 78
Kruschev, Nikita, 29, 78
   on Cuban Communism, 27
   and the Missile Crisis, 38

La Coubre, 30
La Plata, Battle of, 21
Latin America, and Cuba, 57
Literacy Campaign, 33f; **34, 35**

M26J, the July 26th Movement, 14, 17, 82
Maceo, Antonio (The Bronze Titan), 24, 78
machismo, 68, 82
Mafia, 61
Manley Michael, 62, 79
Marti, José, 11, 13, 16, 79
Marx, Karl, 52
mass organizations, 54
Matanzas, and People's Power, 55
Mathews, Herbert, 22
Mexico, 17f
Mikoyan, Anastas, 29, 30, 79; **38**
"millionaires", 50
Missile Crisis, 35ff; **36**
Moncada, attack on, 10ff; **12**
"Moncada Manifesto", 11, 82
"Moncadistas", 13, 54, 82
Movement of Non-Aligned Countries, 64, 83

New Man, and Woman, 47f
New York Times, 22, 29

nickel, 28
Niquero, 19
Nixon, Richard M., 29
   and CIA, 30
   election statements on Cuba, 30
   lack of sympathy for Cuba, 59
   Watergate, 60

October Crisis, *see* Missile Crisis
Organization of American States (OAS), 57, 83
Oriente, 8, 10, 19, 21
Orthodox Party, 8, 9, 83

Pais, Frank, 19, 79
"Patriotic Clubs of the 26th July", 18
People's Power, 55, 83
   Assemblies, 56
Pines, Isle of (now Isle of Youth), 15, 16
Playa Giron (Bay of Pigs), 30ff, 83
Poder Popular, *see* People's Power
Presidential Palace, attack on, 22
Prio Soccaras, Carlos, 18, 79

Radio Rebelde, 23, 25, 83
Radio Reloj, 23
Reagan, Ronald, 62
Revolution, export of, 44ff
Revolutionary Directorate (DR), 22, 82

Santamaria, Abel, 11, 80
Santiago de Cuba, 10, 11, 12, 16, 25
Schools in the Countryside, 65ff, 84; **66**
Seaga, Edward, 62
Siboney, 11, 13
Sierra Maestra, 10, 19f, 23, 24, 29, 84
Soto, Lionel, 8
Spanish, Cuba's war of independence from, 8, 13, 84

sport, 67, 68
Stevenson, Adlai, 31, 80
sugar, 30, 39, 40
   10 Million Ton Harvest, 48ff

Ten Million Tons, *see* sugar
Third World, and Cuba, 61f
Trujillo, Rafael Leonidas, 8, 80
Turquino Peak, 19; **21**

U2, 35, 84
United Nations, General Assembly, 27, 28, 64f
   Cuban demands at UN, 31
United States of America
   Ambassador at UN on the Bay of Pigs, 31
   attacks on Cuba, 28, 29, 59
   Cuban relations, 27, 28, 57ff
   cuts Cuban sugar quotas, 30, 49
   Guatemala plot, 30
   "Interest Section", 59
   invasion plans, 30
   Senate Sub-Committee on assassinations, 60
USSR/Cuban diplomatic & economic relations, 29
   economic agreements, 30
   USA/USSR agreement, 38

Valdes, Ramiro, 18, 80
Venceremos Brigade, 50

Wall Street Journal, on Fidel Castro's prestige, 30
   on CIA invasion plans, 30f
women's rights, 68

Zafra, 50, 84